HOW TO LIVE
Though An
EXECUTIVE

HOW TO LIVE
Though An
EXECUTIVE

L. RON HUBBARD

PUBLICATIONS, INC.

A HUBBARD PUBLICATION

Published in the United States by
Bridge Publications, Inc.
4751 Fountain Avenue
Los Angeles, California 90029

ISBN 0-88404-448-3

Published in other countries by
NEW ERA® Publications International, ApS
Store Kongensgade 55
1264 Copenhagen K, Denmark

ISBN 87-7336-642-0

Printed in the United States of America

Important Note

In reading this book, be very certain you never go past a word you do not fully understand.

The only reason a person gives up a study or becomes confused or unable to learn is because he or she has gone past a word that was not understood.

The confusion or inability to grasp or learn comes AFTER a word that the person did not have defined and understood.

Have you ever had the experience of coming to the end of a page and realizing you didn't know what you had read? Well, somewhere earlier on that page you went past a word that you had no definition for or an incorrect definition for.

Here's an example. "It was found that when the crepuscule arrived the children were quieter and when it was not present, they were much livelier." You see what happens. You think you don't understand the whole idea, but the inability to understand came entirely from the one word you could not define, *crepuscule*, which means twilight or darkness.

It may not only be the new and unusual words that you will

have to look up. Some commonly used words can often be misdefined and so cause confusion.

This datum about not going past an undefined word is the most important fact in the whole subject of study. Every subject you have taken up and abandoned had its words which you failed to get defined.

Therefore, in studying this book be very, very certain you never go past a word you do not fully understand. If the material becomes confusing or you can't seem to grasp it, there will be a word just earlier that you have not understood. Don't go any further, but go back to BEFORE you got into trouble, find the misunderstood word and get it defined.

Definitions

As an aid to the reader, words most likely to be misunderstood have been defined in footnotes the first time they occur in the text. Words sometimes have several meanings. The footnote definitions in this book only give the meaning that the word has as it is used in the text. Other definitions for the word can be found in a dictionary.

A glossary including all the footnote definitions is at the back of this book.

Introduction

The experience of L. Ron Hubbard in the handling and organizing of communications[1] and communications systems is extensive. Educated in mathematics and engineering at George Washington University, he early became interested in problems of human relationships and the applications of electronics thereto. He has studied and worked in several different systems of communications in order to bring the system described here to perfection. Such systems included: the United States Army Signal Corps,[2] the Marine Corps system, the merchant marine system (including the British and Netherlands variations and wartime practices and refinements), US Government communications systems, US Navy systems (including letter mail, filing,

---

1. **communications:** means of sending messages, orders, etc., including telegraph, telephone, radio and television. The definition of *communication* is the interchange of ideas across space. Its full definition is the consideration and action of impelling an impulse or particle from source-point across a distance to receipt-point, with the intention of bringing into being at the receipt-point a duplication and understanding of that which emanated from the source-point. The formula of communication is cause, distance, effect, with intention, attention and duplication with understanding.

2. **United States Army Signal Corps:** a branch of the army responsible for military communications, meteorological studies and related work.

radio, codes, networks for amphibious[3] landings, and, most complex of all, combat information centers,[4] as in the handling of fighter planes from carriers and in submarine search and destruction). The more beneficial points of these systems have been utilized, and their obvious and glaring mistakes have been avoided.

In his study of business and organizational communications systems, both interoffice and interplant, Mr. Hubbard has discovered that much is still to be desired to produce in these even a rudimentary circulation of information. His calculations demonstrate that by reason of poor communications alone most business and industrial organizations[5] are running at less than 12 percent efficiency. Additionally, the most valuable personnel in American business are being wasted by improper communications service. Their time is spent largely in efforts to communicate and to obtain compliance with their plans and orders.

---

3. **amphibious:** designating, of or for a military operation involving the landing of assault troops on a shore from seaborne transports.

4. **combat information centers:** agencies found on most major combat vessels which coordinate the activities of naval departments and divisions during preparations for battle and in actual battle (abbreviated *CIC*). CIC is the sensory center of the ship, the place in which tactical information is gathered and evaluated, and action coordinated. Specifically, CIC is charged with the responsibility of gathering all possible information concerning friendly or enemy ships or aircraft within range of the equipment, evaluating this information, delivering parts of the evaluated information to appropriate stations aboard ship and controlling tactical units.

5. **organizations:** numbers of persons or groups having specific responsibilities and united for some purpose or work; numbers of terminals and communication lines united with a common purpose. The purpose keeps in contact with one another the terminals and the lines. An organization isn't a factory or a house. It isn't a machine or a product. It is something which has its own spirit. It is composed of people who are governed by certain rules and purposes and who know how to do their jobs.

Recognizing that the role of the executive[6] is planning and supervision, Mr. Hubbard, after a survey of many organizations, originated and composed the system which is outlined in this book. He had two chief objects in mind. One, to save executives' time and make it possible for them to fill their proper role in an organization. Two, to reduce the confusion amongst employees and workers who, served by inadequate communication channels and methods, can have no clear understanding of the problems and concerns of management.

In addition to the fact that workers are rendered inefficient and confused by misunderstandings about what they are to do, a poor communications system makes it possible for various elements, undesirable alike to worker and manager, to interfere between production and management and create disturbances which are reflected in broad and paralyzing strikes. These elements gain their power by denying information to the worker or by perverting information.

It is Mr. Hubbard's concept that anyone in an organization is, to some degree, a manager, whether he manages the whole organization, a small group of people, or simply a file case or a

---

6. **executive:** one who holds a position of administrative or managerial responsibility in an organization. To give one some idea of the power associated with the word, Noah Webster, in 1828, defined it as "The officer, whether king, president or other chief magistrate, who superintends the execution of the laws; the person who administers the government, executive power or authority in government." Executive is used in distinction from legislative and judicial. The body that deliberates and enacts laws is legislative; the body that judges or applies the laws to particular cases is judicial; the body or person who carries the laws into effect or superintends the enforcement of them is executive, according to its nineteenth-century governmental meaning according to Webster. The word comes from the Latin "Ex(s)equi (past participle ex[s]ecutus), execute, follow to the end: ex-, completely + sequi, to follow." In other words, he follows things to the end and *gets something done*.

machine. Each, with his responsibility, is part of the neurone[7] or nerve system of the organization, and he cannot function without clear and adequate instructions. Nor can he function unless he can obtain cooperation.

Far from opposing associations of employees, Mr. Hubbard sees in these one of the few attempts to improve the circumstances and function of the worker. In his view, anything undesirable which has arisen around such associations derives immediately from the inability of the worker, under present systems, to maintain adequate two-way communication[8] with those who are making it possible for him to have a job to do.

The severance of communication renders the worker anxious and confused, and he becomes open to suggestion that he is not and never can be a managing part of the organization for which he works and must, therefore, exist under a constant state of cold or hot war with upper management.

The worker feels that he can only revolt against sources of command which he cannot reach and which, using poor systems of communication, rarely reach him.

After broad study in this field, Mr. Hubbard developed the system presented here. He used, in particular, his knowledge of the human mind and its functioning under optimum and nonoptimum conditions, as covered in Scientology. Scientology means *scio*, knowing in the fullest sense of the word and *logos*,

---

7. **neurone:** individual cell of the nervous system which, though effectively in contact with other nerve cells, is a structurally distinct unit; used figuratively to describe the functioning and communication of an individual within a larger group.

8. **two-way communication:** the normal cycle of a communication between two people, which works as follows: Joe, having originated a communication, and having completed it, may then wait for Bill to originate a communication to Joe, thus completing the remainder of the two-way cycle of communication.

study. In itself the word means literally *knowing how to know*. Scientology encompasses a knowledge of the mind and spirit which can be applied to improve conditions in many different aspects of life.

Treating business as an organism, it is discovered to be either sick or well in direct ratio to the inability or ability of its communications system to carry orders, execution and information throughout its entire body.

In the opinion of many who have studied and applied L. Ron Hubbard's system of communications, we face now an inevitable constructive revolution in plant management and national production.

—The Editors

Contents

1

The Oxcart of Modern Planning

1

The Oxcart of Modern Planning

The subject of communications has not been thoroughly investigated at any time by any man. Only now do we begin to investigate it and to formulate the principles and practices of communication. It is expected that this study will result in the creation of a profession of communicators,[1] which will serve industry, commerce and government to make communications flow.

Communications could be said to be the study and practice of interchanging ideas, individual to individual, individual to group, group to individual and group to group. It has not been understood clearly in the past that the failure of a group to communicate ideas within itself results in the failure of the group; that the failure of communication between the group and its leader results in the failure of leadership. Uniformly, throughout

---

1. **communicators:** those who keep communication lines moving or controlled for an executive. The communicator is to help the executive free his or her time for essential income earning actions, rest or recreation, and to prolong the term of appointment of the executive by safeguarding against overload. The communicator's job includes more than secretarial duties, as the communicator is responsible for policing unusual and unnecessary traffic on the executive's lines and for ensuring that the executive's orders are complied with.

industry and commerce, breakdowns which are blamed on poor leadership, insubordination[2] or general ineptness[3] may be attributed correctly to failures of communication.

The leader and his subordinates wish to work smoothly together. They are often skilled at the operations which they must estimate and perform. But, lacking a cultural heritage of good communication, they find themselves unable in many cases to use their skills effectively. Not realizing what it is they lack, they blame each other's abilities and motives and so create discord and further failure of communication.

Ideas newly developed and organized in Scientology have illuminated the subject of communication as never before. There is a clear parallel, in the field of communication, between the individual and the group. With poor communication, the individual is not sane, the group is not effective. With no communication, the individual is dead, the group disbands.

We have learned that an individual who cannot communicate with his own past, through memory, is at a great disadvantage; and an individual who cannot communicate with the present, through perception, is helpless, being unable to estimate the efforts required for meeting and creating the future. Communication within the individual is essential and indispensable. Lacking memory, which is communication with the past, and perception, which is communication with the present, the individual cannot plan a course of action. He cannot deal with his own problems. He is considered insane. So it is with groups, also.

---

2. **insubordination:** resistance to or defiance of authority; refusal to obey orders; disobedience.

3. **ineptness:** lack of skill or aptitude for a particular task or assignment; awkwardness; clumsiness.

In an organization which has poor communications, management cannot plan. The function of management is planning, but management cannot perform this function. Of course, an executive can go through the motions of planning. He can hold meetings, discussions, conferences endlessly. He can issue orders. He can talk about planning. But unless he is in real communication with his organization, unless the reports he receives reflect actual events and processes, and reflect them all, he is planning in a vacuum. His plans will not be carried out because they will not be appropriate. They will not be carried out because with such poor communication they will not even be received. Nothing will function in this organization without good communication.

What has passed in our society for good communication, however, is on a level with oxcart travel over trackless deserts and mountain wastes. The primitive communications systems which we use cannot carry the load, either in adequate volume or with sufficient speed. While transport of material has jumped from the sailing ship to the jet plane, communications have advanced only to the equivalent of Fulton's[4] steamboat. Telephone, telegraph, radio, duplicators, airmail and television may deceive us into thinking that communications is developed appropriately for our age. But these are only mechanical aids. They are not communications. Far more important than communicating *devices* are communicating *people* and communicating *practices*.

The technology of communications is not to be confused with the technology of building, maintaining and operating communication machines. The technology of communications deals with the interchange of ideas. It deals with the nature of thought within the individual and within the group. Its unit of

---

4. **Fulton:** Robert Fulton (1765–1815), American engineer and inventor; builder of the first profitable steamboat.

operation is not a machine but a human being. In an organization the size of a small factory, an almost perfect communications system could be instituted without the use of any material technology more complicated than pencils, paper, sheets of carbon paper and some racks and filing cabinets. But the individuals operating this system would have to know more about the subject of communications than all the telephone, telegraph, radio, Wirephoto[5] and television operators, builders and maintainers in the world put together. Conversely, an organization of moderate size might have at its disposal every conceivable communication device—recorders, telephones, duplicating equipment, mimeograph machines,[6] electronic computers and any other ingenious and fascinating device—and still be 90 percent ineffective in communication. And this often happens.

Scientology has revealed an important fact in relation to a communications system: A person's position on the Tone Scale[7] regulates what his stand on communication will be. An individual who is angry will reverse the truth, turn black into white. A covert[8] individual will alter the truth as much as he can

5. **Wirephoto:** (*trademark*) a device for transmitting photographs over distances by wire, as in a telegraph system.

6. **mimeograph machines:** duplicating machines for producing copies from a stencil.

7. **Tone Scale:** a scale, in Scientology, which shows the emotional tones of a person. These, ranged from the highest to the lowest, are, in part, serenity, enthusiasm (as we proceed downward), conservatism, boredom, antagonism, anger, covert hostility, fear, grief, apathy. An arbitrary numerical value is given to each level on the scale. (*See Appendix, page 133.*) There are many aspects of the Tone Scale and using it makes possible the prediction of human behavior. For further information on the Tone Scale, read the book *Science of Survival* by L. Ron Hubbard.

8. **covert:** characterized by concealed, hidden or disguised hostility; referring to a person at the level of *covert hostility* on the Tone Scale. (*See Appendix, page 133.*) Such an individual can be accurately spotted by his conversation, since he seeks only to enturbulate those around him, to upset them by his conversation, to destroy them without their ever being aware of his purpose. He listens only to data which will serve him in his enturbulations. Here is the gossip, here is the unfaithful wife, here is the card cheat; here is the most undesirable stratum of any social order. *See also* **Tone Scale** and **enturbulated** in the glossary.

without being detected. An apathetic individual will fail to pass any communications except those which carry an apathetic and hopeless message. As an individual rises on the Tone Scale, he communicates better and better. His communications are more and more direct, accurate and constructive. The line,[9] in other words, is carrying more and more theta.[10] As an individual falls away from a high position on the Tone Scale, he communicates worse and worse. His communications are less and less open, honest and useful. The line is carrying more and more entheta.[11]

If we know that a man is angry when he is telling us something, we can evaluate his communication as less truthful than if he were merely bored. If we know that he is afraid, we can discount his communication almost entirely. When he returns to a higher level, however, we can again consider his communications valuable. If he does not return to a higher level, we are justified in not communicating with him, unless it be with the purpose of bringing him back to a higher level. For the sake of the communications system, either he must be brought to a higher level or the communication line to him must be cut. A

---

9. **line:** the route along which particles travel between one terminal and the next in an organization; a fixed pattern of terminals who originate and receive or receive and relay orders, information or other particles. A line can be vertical such as a command line where authority and power of position increases the higher up one goes, or a line can be horizontal where each terminal on the line shares a similar status. *See also* **terminal** in the glossary.

10. **theta:** energy peculiar to life which acts upon material in the physical universe and animates it, mobilizes it and changes it; natural creative energy of a being which he has free to direct toward survival goals, especially when it manifests itself as useful, constructive communications. The term comes from the Greek letter *theta* (θ), which the Greeks used to represent *thought* or perhaps *spirit*. The broad definition of *theta* as used in Scientology is thought, life force, *élan vital*, the spirit, the soul.

11. **entheta:** a coined word in Scientology, made from the words *enturbulated theta* (thought or life). As used here, it refers to communications which, based on lies and confusions, are slanderous, choppy or destructive in an attempt to overwhelm or suppress a person or group. *See also* **enturbulated** and **theta** in the glossary.

communicator at a low tone[12] level is far more destructive than a teletype which prints "Nxw xs thx txmx fxr xll gxxd mxn tx cxmx tx thx xxd xf thx pxrty."[13] We would not think of leaving such a machine in the circuit. Far less should we think of leaving a frightened or angry communicator in the system.

The tone of a group can be measured by its level of communication. If it communicates well within itself, its tone must be high. If its communication is faulty, its tone is not so high. If its communication is perverted, it is a sick organization. If its communication ceases, it dies.

The job of estimating the tone of a group is not begun by talking with the management or by watching the individual workmen at their skills. It may be assumed that the management knows something about the business and that the workmen are able to do their jobs. The investigation will be most rapid and valid if the communications system of the group is examined— for this is the nervous system of the group. A group with good communications will not be handicapped seriously by the presence of a few dolts.[14] A group with poor communications cannot succeed even if it contains intellectual giants.

The tone level of a group can be raised, as if magically, by the introduction of a genuine communicator. The communicator enters into the operation of the group with the sole purpose of establishing and maintaining good communication lines. He does not concern himself with the conduct or skill of individuals

---

12. **tone:** a level of emotion as given on the Tone Scale. *See also* **Tone Scale** in the glossary.

13. **Nxw xs thx. . . . :** an example illustrating an inoperational teletype, using the common typist's practice exercise, "Now is the time for all good men to come to the aid of the party."

14. **dolts:** dull, stupid people; blockheads.

in the organization except as they relate to communications. He insists that a certain procedure of communication be followed. When this procedure begins to operate, the tone of the group automatically rises, the work goes better, there is less waste, there is more cooperation. Nothing need be said about work, waste or cooperation. All that is necessary is that the communication procedure be carried out. This is a big job, but it can be done.

The tone level of the communicator in regard to matters other than communications, while important, can be partly compensated for by education in communications. He might be covert on the subject of sex and angry on the subject of politics and bored on the subject of religion and still be an effective communicator—provided he did not have to deal with any messages on the subjects of sex, politics or religion. If he did have to deal with these subjects, we might expect his training and practice in good communication to overcome to a considerable degree his inclination to handle these messages in a low-toned manner. It is probable, and more than probable, that continued operation as a good communicator would bring him slowly up the Tone Scale in general.

Therefore, it is not necessary for the communicator to be far above normal as an individual, although his knowledge of communication will place him very far above normal in this vital and pervasive function and render him extremely important and helpful to the group. He or she must only desire to keep the lines up, to see communications flow, to see the system operate as it has been designed to operate, and to prevent any interference with that operation.

The job of the communicator will be as arduous as the tone of the group is low. It will be as easy as the tone of the group is high. But, as the communicator does his job, the tone of the group will rise.

A group which is low-toned will curse and threaten the communicator. The personnel of a naval vessel, where the tone is usually low, will constantly rave and rant at the communications people. The communicator is on the spot. Those members of the organization who are doing the planning are angry at him because he can't handle their needs fast enough. Those members of the organization who are authoritarians[15] call him on the carpet[16] for daring to communicate anything at all. He is in a constant dilemma between so-called security and getting something done. He must adjust his operations to carry the most theta communications he can, using the time, equipment, technology, personnel and authoritarian restrictions which have been handed to him. The little he knows about communications he has learned through his own experience. Those whom he serves know even less. They have no conception of his proper function. They think of him as a communicating *machine*, subject to their will. And yet, in spite of all this, they have a peculiar respect for him—a respect which is inherited from the past.

Always, communicators have been sacred people because communication lines have been sacred. A society which has any organization or advancement holds its communication lines sacred, or it loses its organization and advancement. The priest derives his sacredness from his function as a communications point: He stands between the people and their deity[17] and relays messages both ways. He is not the god. He does not own the god. But he controls the communication line to the god. Any individuals in that society who felt that they had their own communication line to the god would no longer hold the priest sacred.

---

15. **authoritarians:** persons who advocate, practice or enforce unquestioning obedience to authority, as that of a dictator, rather than individual freedom of judgment and action.

16. **carpet, on the:** in the position of being reprimanded by one in authority.

17. **deity:** god or goddess.

In the university, the great authority on sponges is important because he stands between his students and a vast number of books on sponges. If all the knowledge on sponges were contained in one medium-sized volume, the students could read it, and the great authority would no longer have any importance. In order to prevent this, or anything like it, from happening, the great authority makes it clear to the students that there are a *great* many books on sponges, that the knowledge in them is diverse and conflicting, that only he has read them all, and that students are congenitally[18] incapable of understanding them anyway. If, on the other hand, the great authority understands his job, he relays all he knows about sponges as simply as he can. He may be so good at relaying information that he is considered a great professor. This means that he is a great communicator. Only rarely does he originate or discover any material about sponges. Only rarely is he a creative man or a discoverer. But, from time to time, he is a good communicator, and when he is, he is loved by his students and envied by his colleagues.

A man on a communications post[19] who will relay all material, who will alter it only to make it more understandable, who will delay it only if it is incomplete and soon to be completed, and who will break off the line if, and only if, it is entheta and destructive, is a man who will do well as a communicator. A communicator does not confuse himself with the goal-making[20] section, the planning section or the production section. His function reaches into all of these, but only to communicate, not

---

18. **congenitally:** as the result of a condition present at birth, whether inherited or caused by the environment, especially the uterine environment.

19. **post:** a position, job or duty to which a person is assigned or appointed; an assigned area of responsibility and action in an organization which is supervised in part by an executive.

20. **goal-making:** creating or establishing the aims, achievements or ends toward which effort is directed.

to usurp[21] the activities of any section of the organization.

Some men originate new ideas. Often they are poor communicators. The communicator who is assigned to such an individual has the same problem as the professor who is interpreting a vast library of books to students. The communicator must express what this creative man is doing. He must require the creative man to give him the material in a form which can be understood by all the people who are on the communication line. He must understand what the creative man is talking about before he can communicate any of it to others. This makes the communicator for such a creative point a very important person. Translating the cryptic[22] utterances of the genius who is absorbed in the creation of an idea is a full time job. Sometimes the genius acts as his own communicator. Sometimes he is a genius at communicating. But more often he is a genius at designing something which no one understands and about which he communicates very poorly. A communicator assigned full time to doing nothing but understanding what this man is about and communicating on the subject to others is a necessity in such a case.

When the communicator is dealing with a planning management, the difficulty of translation is not so great, but the volume is very large. A manager is constantly giving out orders, at all hours of the day and night. The business tycoon,[23] who works at his job twenty-four hours a day, might well wear out three or four communicators in the course of one day. If four communicators were assigned to follow him around in six-hour shifts, the saving of his time and energy and the realization of his ideas would pay their salary a hundred times over. The manager would always be in communication with his organization, but he

---

21. **usurp:** appropriate wrongly to oneself (a right, prerogative, etc.).

22. **cryptic:** mysterious in meaning; puzzling; ambiguous.

23. **tycoon:** a businessperson of great wealth and power.

would never have to *worry* about communication. Normally, a manager is seldom in communication with his organization and he is always worried about communication.

Management exists to make plans. Management does not exist to communicate. That is the communicator's job. Most management spends 90 percent of its time communicating and 10 percent making plans. If management did not have to think about communication, it could be ten times as free to plan. The communicator's job is not only to insist that management communicate, but also to participate in the activities of management as an observer, so that anything which needs to be communicated can be communicated without management even having to think about it.

One prime necessity exists before this can happen. Management must trust and have confidence in the communicator and the communications system. The communicator of the head of a big industry must know as much about that industry as the head man himself. This does not mean that the communicator should be capable of running the industry. It means that he should be familiar with all the problems of the industry and particularly familiar with the methods and views of the manager, so that he will know what to communicate and what not to communicate. If the manager does all his thinking out loud, the communicator must know enough not to communicate it. The plant can get along without the manager's feelings about his golf score, his remarks to the new secretary about the charm of her figure, his nebulous[24] desires to run the competition out of business, his worries about the encroachments[25] of

---

24. **nebulous:** lacking form; hazy; vague; confused.

25. **encroachments:** intrusions (especially by insidious or gradual advances) on the territory, rights or accustomed sphere of action of others; gradual inroads made or extensions of boundaries at the expense of something else.

collectivism[26] etc., etc. All these things are valuable as information to the manager's communicator, because they help the communicator to know what to communicate and how to evaluate it, but they are not plans for operation, and they do not need to be communicated to the plant as orders, rumors or gossip.

When management gains confidence in the communicator, management will no longer express itself in curt, unexplained, mechanical orders. The manager will think and express himself freely. When, in the course of this thinking, a definite plan is formulated, it will be automatically put into the communications system, and, as will be detailed below, *it will inevitably be carried out or refused openly.* Management, trusting the communications system, will at last be free to plan.

A communicator in a military organization is on the spot because he cannot persuade the generals to trust him. The generals will tell their harlots[27] but not their communicators. Many a battle has been lost because of this dismal fact. The general will not tell his own message center[28] what to tell the troops, because the information is secret. But the plan has already gone out to the enemy through the barrooms.[29] This is known as security. Security is a dangerous thing. It makes an organization irrational by depriving it of data. The best security in communications would be the fastest, fullest communication of all data to all points of reception. The plan would go into action before the

---

26. **collectivism:** the socialistic theory of the collective ownership or control of all the means of production, and especially of the land, by the whole community or state, i.e., the people collectively, for the benefit of the people as a whole. *See also* **socialism** in the glossary.

27. **harlots:** prostitutes.

28. **message center:** an office or other area where incoming and outgoing messages, mail, etc., are received and transmitted as by telephone, computer or messenger.

29. **barrooms:** establishments or rooms with a bar for the serving of alcoholic beverages.

enemy could do anything about it. Only rarely is secrecy the best method of operation. As a general habit of operation, it is disastrous.

The communicator in an organization which has secret goals or secret plans for reaching goals, will have to sacrifice some of the efficiency of the communications system to the end of secrecy. But most organizations have very little need for secrecy if they only knew it. And most of the secrecy in industrial and commercial organizations is dedicated not to the benefit of the operation, but to the advantage of some individual or subgroup. When this kind of secrecy is removed by a communications system, open and honest cooperation is the only *possible* method of operation.

The communicator must know what the goal of the organization is. If he does not know, he cannot function as a communicator, he can only function as a communicating machine, which is not the same thing. The moment management keeps a goal or a plan secret from the communicator, management must again undertake the burden of communications. The usurpation[30] of the function of communication by management is the primary cause of failure in organizational communication. Management can't plan if it communicates because it hasn't time to do both. Management must plan in order to be management. So management does not bother to communicate and will not let anyone else communicate. Very soon management is thoroughly out of communication with the plant.

Often we find an attempt to operate down in the plant, which is carrying on the business of production, practically in the absence of direction by management. The foremen cast doves

---

30. **usurpation:** the act of usurping (wrongly appropriating) another's rights, privileges, etc.; an instance of encroachment on or upon (liberty, etc.).

into the air, or use fortune-telling cards or a Ouija board[31] to find out what management wants to do, and then they pass the word around among the workmen that such and such should be done. When an order finally does arrive from management, it is not in agreement with what the foremen got on their Ouija board. Recriminations,[32] delay, government contracts and general havoc ensue—all because nobody is communicating, nobody is seeing to it that communication of all ideas to all affected persons takes place at all times. This can be done only by a communications system. It cannot be done in odd moments by executives, accountants and lathe[33] operators.

It is a measure of the state of our society that a communicator is thought to be no more than a girl who pounds a teletype or a boy who carries messages. A man's secretary is supposed to do nothing but answer the letters he tells her to answer. She is not supposed to use her brain. But if he is a successful executive, his secretary will be a communicator in the sense in which we are now using the word. She will evaluate what he tells her and see that it gets to the right person at the right time, and she won't bother him about it. He is busy planning. All she asks him to do is give her the right data. He makes plans, she communicates them. That is a working team.

In ancient times, the herald[34] represented the sacredness of

---

31. **Ouija board:** (*trademark*) a device consisting of a small board on legs that rests on a larger board marked with words, letters of the alphabet, etc., and that by moving over the larger board and touching the words, letters, etc., while the fingers of spiritualists, mediums, or others rest lightly upon it, is employed to answer questions, give messages, etc.

32. **recriminations:** counter-accusations; accusations brought in turn by the accused against the accuser.

33. **lathe:** a machine for shaping an article of wood, metal, etc., by holding and turning it rapidly against the edge of a cutting or abrading tool.

34. **herald:** (formerly) a royal or official messenger, especially one representing a monarch in an ambassadorial capacity during wartime.

communication. There was a herald's college. Heralds had degrees. They could travel anywhere. Much falderol[35] was attendant[36] upon their calling.[37] A spurious[38] herald could be detected quickly by a genuine herald. No one but a herald could communicate between two forces. He arrived with his white flag (now degraded into a symbol of surrender) and he was safe no matter what message he carried because his person was sacred.

In these days, communications is not a specialized profession. What is called communications is merely the operation, maintenance and development of machines to assist the communicator. But there is no communicator. It is significant that great technology exists for the physical transfer of communications from one place to another, but no technology exists for the creation of the communications themselves.

---

35. **falderol:** mere nonsense; foolish talk or ideas.

36. **attendant:** accompanying as a circumstance or result.

37. **calling:** one's occupation, profession or trade.

38. **spurious:** not genuine, authentic or true; not from the claimed, pretended or proper source; counterfeit.

2

Why Organizations Act Psychotic

2

Why Organizations
Act Psychotic[1]

Communication lines have some interesting properties.
They have, one might say, life and powers of their own.

A strong, theta (reason bearing) communication line has
a way of maintaining its own life and defending itself from
interference. If it is tampered with, it will blow up at the point
where it is interrupted, and it will blow up the person who
interrupts it. Any person who will interrupt a line which is
carrying smooth, reasonable, well-organized, theta material
must be acting on a suicidal compulsion, because the people
who are dependent upon this line will take strong measures to
preserve and protect it. Even if they never have been told anything about communications as science or art, the value of a
communication line is implicit[2] in every operation of theta,
within the individual or within the group. If a man stands across

---

1. **psychotic:** characterized by or afflicted with psychosis. A *psychosis,* per psychiatry,
is any major form of mental affliction or disease. In Scientology, a *psychotic* is classified as a person who is physically or mentally harmful to those about him out of
proportion to the amount of use he is to them. Used figuratively in this sense.

2. **implicit:** necessarily or naturally involved though not plainly apparent or expressed; essentially a part or condition; inherent.

---

a strong communication line and blocks its flow,[3] it will blow up in his face.

If the line is not so strong, the individual may succeed in blocking it. The communicator, wishing to restore this line to operation, need only demonstrate that the line was interrupted by this individual. The individual will then blow off the line and, quite possibly, out of the organization completely. Wherever there is a person who will pervert a communication line, there is a germ of death in the organization. If the organization contains much life, it will not tolerate such an infection.

If the organization contains but little life, however, a clever authoritarian may sit on the communication lines indefinitely, perverting them just enough for his purposes but not enough to cut them completely. If this authoritarian happens to be the head man, the result will be that atmosphere of oppression, uncertainty and rebellion so familiar to the employees and associates of that familiar figure of American business, the self-made tyrant.[4]

Management which has tasted the pleasures of creative planning will have no further time for, nor patience with, the puny powers which can be derived from perverting communications within an organization. A good communications system permits management to be the rider of a racehorse. A poor communications system gives management only the doubtful joys of driving a stubborn mule.

Communication lines are interrupted more frequently by negligence than by design. People are just too busy to follow the

---

3. **flow:** a progress of energy between two points; an impulse or direction of energy particles or thought or masses between terminals; the progress of particles or impulse waves from Point A to Point B.

4. **tyrant:** any person who exercises authority in an oppressive manner; cruel master.

required communication procedures. They neglect to make the slight extra motion which is necessary for their data to be entered properly into the communications system. Or, if there is not yet such a system, they neglect even to tell anyone what they want done or what they have done. The chief communicator in any industry which is instituting a communications system will spend most of his time indoctrinating[5] people in the procedures and reminding them to use the procedures. He will have to persuade them that it is necessary to do this, not because somebody demands it, but because the organization cannot function or live without it.

The communications system is designed to pick up and preserve bits of information such as "The key to the back door of warehouse number three has disappeared," or "There is an unclaimed box of roller bearings[6] in the dispensary,"[7] or "The drinking water in the women's restroom is slightly radioactive," and keep them moving until something is done about them, and then keep them on file for reference in the future. An item like "The key, etc." would be shunted[8] around by the communications system feverishly until the lock was changed and new keys issued. Of course, the communications system would not issue any *orders* about this. It would merely present the information to command points until an order was issued.

The stream of orders which issues from any command point in a large organization is made up of many small items. These items are the minute-to-minute thoughts of the organization.

---

5. **indoctrinating:** instructing; teaching.

6. **roller bearings:** a system used in a machine in which a shaft turns with rollers, generally of steel, arranged in a ringlike track; used to reduce friction.

7. **dispensary:** a place where something is dealt out or distributed, especially medicines.

8. **shunted:** switched to another route or place.

The communications system is the vehicle for these thoughts; it is the nervous system of the group.

We have often compared an organization to a life organism. We can carry this analogy further, to state that an organization without a communications system is like a sponge: insensitive, immobile and helpless. The higher forms of life have highly developed nervous systems, by which all parts of the organism are in communication with each other. If an organism's nervous system is not arranged so that it can feel pain, it cannot withdraw from, nor cope with, danger. Its survival potential is low. If it wishes to attack, it must be in immediate and dependable communication with all its members. Its ability to attack and defend, and thus its survival, are directly dependent upon communication.

A communications system is not only the nervous system but also the brain of an organization—that is, it forms the medium, the mass of tissue through which the planning mind of the organization (all those individuals who originate plans, from the greatest to the smallest) operates. A mind cannot operate without memory. Whether that mind is running an organism or an organization, it must be able to communicate with its past. Memory is absolutely essential to the operation of an organization. An organization with a bad filing system acts psychotic. The filing system, being the memory of the organization, is an integral[9] part of the communications system, which is the brain of the organization. The two cannot be separated, or psychotic behavior will be manifested by the organization.

Management cannot plan without an excellent memory operating in the organization. This memory should not have to be

---

9. **integral:** necessary for completeness; essential.

and, indeed, cannot be enclosed in the heads of one or two individuals. It has to be available to all of the computing and planning levels of the organization. It has to be accurate. The evaluation of the information in it must be exact and uncolored. The organization becomes neurotic[10] to the degree that the information in its memory is colored.

The survival of an organization depends upon its ability to perceive, to compute and to remember. All these take place within the tissues that form the communications system. A group, like an individual, must know what it has done, what it is doing and what it intends to do. A group, like an individual, must have this data available immediately, at will. The more closely a communications system (including perception, memory, estimation of future efforts and relay of orders) approximates the operation of the human mind, the better the organization will function. When the memory of the organization is resident only in the minds of a few individuals, that organization is not functioning as a group, and has no real group memory, but is only borrowing the memories of these individuals in lieu of[11] having a memory of its own. This is highly unsatisfactory. As with an individual, so with a group there is a direct relationship between sanity and ability to communicate with records of the past, as well as with perceptions of the present.

Communication lines also have weaknesses.

A communication line can be cut or interrupted or invalidated in five ways.

---

10. **neurotic:** exhibiting behavior characteristic of one who is insane or disturbed on some subject (as opposed to a psychotic, who is just insane in general).

11. **in lieu of:** in place of; instead of.

The first way is simply to cut the line, to prevent any information from traveling on the line, to pass no despatches.[12]

The second way is to pervert the line, to alter the communications which are going on the line.

The third way is to select all constructive messages out of the line and leave all destructive messages on the line. This is cutting the line by censorship.

The fourth way is to introduce destructive material into the line, to load the line with entheta.

The fifth way is to glut[13] the line, to permit any and all material to go over it, with no selectivity. Those who are on the receiving end will get so much material to deal with that they will become careless and irresponsible in their handling of the material.

Of course, the most successful way to prevent communications from occurring is not to establish a communication line in the first place. This is what usually happens. But if one is established, it can be destroyed by cutting it, by perverting it, by censoring the theta, by introducing entheta or by glutting the line.

There are at least three ways to glut the line. One is to fail to evaluate despatches as to importance and velocity, in a system where traffic is heavy. The receiver then has to read everything to find out which item to handle first. Another way is to permit

---

12. **despatches:** written messages, particularly official communications.

13. **glut:** fill (a receptacle, channel, pipe, etc.) to excess; choke up; saturate thoroughly with some substance.

messages to be verbose,[14] with much talk and little data. Another way is to save up a great amount of material and then send it all at once—to send nothing for five days and then send 100,000 words and then nothing for five days. The receiver has so much to do all at once that he will tend to devaluate the communication in general. If a communicator carelessly lets two months' worth of material on a certain subject pile up on his desk and then releases it all at once, people will be so stunned by the great volume that they will pay no attention to it, and the material may be lost.

A communicator, because he is a communicator, will want lines not to be cut in any of these ways. He will have to know how to prevent their being cut, and the first ability that he will need in order to prevent their being cut will be the ability to evaluate the material that goes over the line. Some items will be very important, some not so important. They must be evaluated. Some items, whether important or not, will have to be done right away if they are to be done at all—they will have, in other words, a high velocity. They must be so evaluated by the communicator. The importance and velocity of every message must be written on it by the communicator, so that the receiver, if he has a pile of a hundred messages, will know which to handle first and which to follow up the most frequently.

In order to be able to evaluate messages in this way, the communicator must know as much about the operation of the organization as the man who is sending the order. He must make his own evaluation of the message. The man who is sending the order may say to the communicator, "This order for orchids for my wife is a top priority, top velocity message. Mark it that way and send it out immediately." It is all right for the executive to say this, but it is not all right for the communicator

---

14. **verbose:** using or containing too many words; wordy; long-winded.

to comply with his request—unless the order really is top priority and a big rush. It is up to the communicator to decide how this message will be communicated. He will probably rate it high velocity, if the orchids are to arrive that night—but he will undoubtedly rate it *low importance.* This will mean to the communications system that if other work is not too pressing, orchids should be purchased for Mrs. Executive that afternoon—or not at all, since there may well be a time limit marked on the message, "before 5:00 P.M.," or something of the sort.

If an executive tries to force his evaluation of an order on the communicator, or if he will not let the communicator know how the order relates to the rest of the operation, or if he generally hides information from the communicator, the communications system, by just that much, will cease to operate properly and communications will begin to fail. Whenever an executive acts as though the communicator were not good enough or trustworthy enough to know about something, the executive will be cutting a communication line, because he will be depriving the communicator of the data he needs to be able to *evaluate* the material which the executive deigns[15] to give him.

An order which was the most important thing that this executive could think of might not be the most important thing that could happen in the organization. It would be up to the communicator of that executive to know the importance of the order in relation to everything that was being handled by the communications system. If he didn't know, it would be up to him to ask the central communications office to evaluate it for him. The communicator is interested in the executive's opinion of the importance of this message. He may even concur with it. But he may not. And the communicator's opinion is the one that counts.

---

15. **deigns:** thinks it worthy of oneself (to do something); thinks fit; condescends.

In a low-toned organization, executives from the head jani-tor on up will try to keep everything a secret. This will make it difficult for the communications system to evaluate their commu-nications. The number of items which have to be classified for security in an organization which has constructive and creative goals and plans should be very small. Sometimes, in such an organization, we find an individual from whose desk there is a niagara[16] of secret and confidential communications. Everything this individual sends out must be delivered in person, must be delivered only to the addressee, is sealed with wax, and must only be sent by a special, trusted messenger. Open one of these messages and you find,

"Joe,

"Will you come over to my office for a closed conference?

"Bill."

It is so secret, he cannot even say it in a secret communica-tion. This individual is accomplishing only one thing with all this secrecy. He is causing whatever meager communication lines there are in the organization to fail. Everything which is kept secret becomes an unknown in the equation which is set up to evaluate and expedite communications. Only a few of these unknowns are necessary to make correct evaluation impossible. Every order or job which is kept secret will raise the chances of duplication[17] or conflict.

---

16. **niagara:** anything taken as resembling Niagara Falls (the falls of the Niagara River in Canada) in force and relentlessness; avalanche.

17. **duplication:** the action of something being made, done or caused to happen again. Used in this sense to denote unnecessary or wasted motion. In Scientology, *duplication* is also used to describe the action of reproducing something exactly. For example, if Person A communicated the concept of a cat to Person B and Person B got the exact same concept of a cat without any alteration, Person B would be said to have *duplicated* what was originated by Person A.

Communicators will have to insist, frequently at first, that people let the communicator know what they are doing—or if they have no communicator on hand in their office, that they act as their own communicator and let the central communications office know what they are doing. If the first vice-president calls up the head painter and tells him to paint the front door of the building red, and the second vice-president calls up the assistant painter and tells him to paint the front door green, there is going to be waste and dissension.[18] But if these two orders come through the communications system, they will bump into each other, and the conflict can be reported and straightened out before the painters get into a fist fight or, at the least, use up a lot of paint and valuable time. When the communicator finds that the vice-president has called the painter on the phone, he will have to remind the vice-president that orders are supposed to go through the communications system. The vice-president may get angry or make fun of the communicator for this. Any organization which cannot cooperate with a communications system is sadly in need of repair. The ease with which a communications system can be assimilated[19] by an organization is a measure of that organization's health.

The new communicator will have to withstand a lot of criticism and "humor" before he establishes himself, even in a fairly healthy organization. The communicator should expect this. If he cannot take it, he cannot function as a communicator. He will have to develop powers of persuasion. He will have to have complete confidence in his profession, and he will have to know it cold. His one advantage will be that he is not under the authority of most of the people with whom he is dealing (although they will not believe this at first and will try to fire him from time to time) and so he will be able to talk to them as an

---

18. **dissension:** strong disagreement; contention or quarrel; discord.

19. **assimilated:** taken in and absorbed or incorporated into the system.

equal. In his inviolability,[20] he can afford to be confident, gracious and helpful even to the most recalcitrant[21] points of the command line.

The communicator is not a messenger. He is a coordinator. He is not in the organization to do everyone's communicating. He is there to help everyone do his own communicating properly. He is an overseer.

---

20. **inviolability:** the quality or fact of being inviolable (not to be treated without proper respect or regard; not liable or allowed to suffer violence).

21. **recalcitrant:** "kicking" against constraint or restriction; obstinately disobedient or rebellious; unmanageable.

3

Evaluation Is of Prime Importance

3

Evaluation Is of Prime Importance

$\mathbf{A}$ communicator deals in facts. One of the most important things he does with facts is evaluate them. The communicator is not running a library, he is running a brain. There is a difference. There are ten million books sitting in libraries today, crammed full of facts. These facts are practically no good to anyone because they have not been evaluated. They show that somebody was very busy collecting facts, but they show nothing else. If we wish to get some good from these facts, we must go into the library and begin to evaluate all the facts we can find on the subject in which we are interested. We must evaluate them against our own experience.

Many fields which pass for science today are little more than vast silos[1] of unevaluated and therefore useless facts. The facts which a communicator must relay and file are meant to be useful at the moment of relay and later whenever they are obtained from the file. Therefore, they must be evaluated.

If Jacqueline, in the business office, orders a new lamb's wool coat through the purchasing department in order to get the

---

1. **silos:** large bins used for the storage of loose materials. Used figuratively in this sense.

company discount, her order will go through the communications system. In the same office, the datum may turn up that the second vice-president is planning to sell the land on which the plant is located. The communicator in that office will have to put both these items on the line. Since he is not building a library, but running a brain, he cannot put both these items on the line with the same evaluation. He will have to give Jacqueline's coat the lowest rating and the vice-president's deal the highest rating. A datum is as important as the number of other data it evaluates. The sale of the land would affect everyone who worked in the plant, all the equipment, all the orders—the whole business, in other words. Jacqueline's coat affects only Jacqueline and somebody in the purchasing department for a brief period. The sale of the land will change all the planning in the organization. Jacqueline's coat will change no planning at all.

Of course, if Jacqueline's coat were mink it might have a greater significance—but the communicator would not care about that. He is not an investigator. He is a communicator. If Jacqueline's coat is mink, that fact will appear in the files, but it will still bear the lowest importance rating. The detective who comes around to find out about Jacqueline and the vice-president may find the coat communication very rewarding. If the detective sends a message to the president about all this, the communicator may care to mark *that* message "important." But the communicator does not take it upon himself to investigate, criticize, correct or assist anyone in the organization about anything but communication.

On the other hand, if the communicator finds that his messages do not get through, he will use every means at his disposal to find out why. When it comes to communication, he is as sensitive to the flow of his lines as an electronic meter, and he is jealous of their continued life and liberty. The communicator has authority on one subject only: communication. When the system fails in any way, he does not rest until it is restored.

In the course of finding out why his communication line is not working, the communicator may uncover a vast plot against the organization. He is not interested in it. The moment he gets his line open again, his work is done. If the line is open—if all lines are open everywhere in the system—the plot will come to light. Someone on the command line will notice it and do something about it. All the communicator has to do is keep the lines open. The communicator does not originate orders or messages on any subject but communication. It is not up to him to pass around his opinions on the state of the organization. That would be an investigator's job.

If someone on the command line were doing a destructive or nonproductive job, that fact would appear in the communications which were filed from that department. The communicator might, if he were not too busy, have an opinion on this individual, but he would not voice it. If, however, this individual failed to answer messages or to send routine reports through on time, the communicator would take every necessary action to correct this—even to a report to the president himself. But if the communicator reported to the president, he would only report that the line to the individual in question had broken down and that he had no way to repair it. He would say nothing about the work of the individual—he would not have to. A failure of communication of that magnitude would show that something was terribly wrong. It would be up to the command line to find out what it was.

A clear distinction must be made between the *importance* of a communication and its *velocity*. Of course, the more important a datum is the higher velocity it may be expected to have; but there will be many exceptions to this.

The most frequent exception will be the order which has a time limit. A car is ordered to meet the incoming representative of the Salt Lake City branch. This representative does not expect to be met; he expects to take a cab; he has always taken a cab; he is used to it; he likes it. Obviously, the importance of this order is small. If it were not carried out, no one would know the difference. On the other hand, the order is given on Tuesday morning at 11:00 A.M. and the plane is due to arrive at 11:28. If this order is to be carried out at all, it must have the highest velocity of which the communications system is capable.

There is, then, no fixed relationship between importance and velocity. From time to time there will be very important data on the line which still will have the lowest velocity: "To the shipping department: If consignment[2] X32 is not out of the state by March 31, the entire plant may be confiscated by the government!" Lowest velocity. Why? Because the date of the order is March 2, and consignment X32 is known to be ready for shipping. This order would be marked *top importance*, but it would not be a rush order. On the other hand, if the date were March 30, we might expect the communicator to take the express elevator to the shipping department and stand there until the shipment went out.

The velocity of a datum depends mainly on the amount of the operation which it will correct or interrupt. If a book is being printed, and a datum turns up which changes the titles of four of the chapters, that datum must be handled as fast as possible. That datum has a higher and higher priority as the moment of starting the presses approaches. After the presses start, it will not be worth stopping them. It will be too late. At that moment, the datum has no priority. It goes back through channels at the usual traffic rate, to make trouble for somebody who gave the order too late. It goes into the files to show who was at fault and what happened. But its velocity is no longer high. It is just a

---

2. **consignment:** a shipment of goods sent to an agent for sale or safekeeping.

record of the fact that the communications system received this order too late.

Many an individual on a command point will overrate his despatches. He will send out positively foolish orders at top velocity. The communicator is not so much interested in how foolish the orders are. His job is to estimate the amount of the operation this order will interrupt. Chances are, if it is so foolish, it will be refused, whether it is top velocity or merely traffic velocity.

If the communicator knows that there is a good reason for refusing this order, he has one course of action open to him— not to block the message or write "Please ignore this!" on the message, but to attach to the message related material from the files which shows that the order is impractical. When he does this, he is running his communications system like a brain. He is aligning the data in the organization's memory with the newly received data, so that the organization can reach a valid decision.

If the order is marked "top velocity" but consists of a request for a dozen toggle bolts to be kept in stock until next year, the communicator will have to reevaluate the velocity. These "top velocity" messages can knock everything else off the line and take up a lot of the system's time and effort. They should not be frequent. The communicator marks "top velocity" off the message with his blue pencil[3] and substitutes "traffic."

The communicator might use three classifications in his grading, based on the degree of change in plans which would be caused by the message. "Operational Interruption" would be the highest classification—or just "Interruption." "Alert" might be

---

3. **blue pencil:** a pencil (traditionally blue), used to make corrections, deletions, etc., as in editing a manuscript.

next. "Traffic" would be the third. Only a few communications would be marked "Alert." Very few would be marked "Interruption." This kind of classification, however, would not distinguish between importance and velocity, and the communicator might decide that it was necessary to distinguish, so he would adopt, probably, a system of numbers and letters.

In various organizations, various grading systems have been used. The kind of grading done depends on the purpose of the grader. In military intelligence operations, information may be graded in terms of the reliability of the informant and the probability which the operative[4] thinks the information has. To paraphrase it, the letters *A* to *D* stand for the reliability of the informant, and the numbers *1* to *5* stand for the probable truth of the information. *A* stands for a person of known integrity who is trained to report on the subject. *B* stands for a person of unknown integrity who is trained. *C* is a person of known integrity who is untrained. And *D* is a person of unknown integrity who is also untrained. The numbers *1* to *5* are diminishing degrees of probability. The number *5* would stand for "impossible." "*D5*," then, would be slang for the worst information an operative could get his hands on: an impossible story from an ignorant liar.

The system which is being described could be cut down for a small organization. Naturally, in an organization of ten persons, a much simpler system would be used. The system which is being described would work for an organization which covers a thousand towns, a thousand military companies, a hundred departments or a government. Anyone in such an organization who wanted to hear from anyone else or have his communications received would have to learn how to communicate through the system. He would have to learn how to make his messages

---

4. **operative:** a secret agent; spy.

terse[5] without leaving out information. If he wrote a ten-page letter to the president or the commanding officer or the chief administrator, reporting an argument with a co-worker and resigning his position, the communicator would simply refuse the message. The communicator would insist that he simplify the message to: "I don't get along with Jones. He is unreasonable. I quit!" The ten-page letter could be kept in the files as a reference and its existence could be noted on the message—or it could be attached to the message as an information sheet, but the communicator cannot permit the message to take such a form that the president will not read it, or will waste time reading it. The communicator has to keep the lines flowing.

Probably the worst type of message which can be sent is the recorded voice. Recordings made on dictating machines sometimes are sent as messages. This kind of message is the perfect example of what can be wrong with a communication. It has every possible fault built into it as an integral and inevitable part of it.

First of all, it is meant to save someone's time, a typist's; but it wastes the time of the person to whom it is sent, who is presumably more important than a typist.

Second, it is an invitation to the sender to be wordy. Whoever heard of sending a recording with only one minute of recording on it? That would be *wasting* the recording, wouldn't it? (Value, several pennies.) So, the sender fills up the recording with friendly chatter—all fifteen minutes of it. Then, at the last minute he thinks of something else he has to say, and turns the recording over. Having done that, he has to fill up that side, too. One-half hour of time for the sender, one-half hour of time for the receiver—a full hour is spent by this organization in

---

5. **terse:** neatly or effectively precise; brief and full of substance or meaning.

communicating ideas which might have been put down on paper in ten minutes and read in one minute!

Third, the recording is blank unless it is played on a machine. This means that it cannot be evaluated anywhere along the line—that it breaks the communication line, in other words.

Fourth, it cannot be filed or cross-indexed. It can only be put away under one subject head, and there it will stay until the end of time or until the building burns down (as the building will, if it is being used by people who would try to communicate with recordings); for who will take it out of the file again? It would have to be played on a machine, and no one has the half hour required to play it.

In other words, such a recording is completely blank to all but the sender and the receiver—and if the receiver is smart, he will not bother to listen to it, either. If an executive has sixteen subordinates, each of whom would send him one recording each day, he would spend eight hours a day listening to recordings which brought him eight minutes' information. A ratio of sixty to one. Of course, since an executive is expected to work at least twenty hours a day, subordinates continue to use recordings.

A principle which the communicator must know is that communications get briefer and better evaluated as they go up toward the top of the command line. They must, or they will not be read when they arrive. Conversely, communications need, usually, to be more detailed as they go down the command line. Instructions have to be full of data in inverse[6] ratio to the receiver's height on the command line.

---

6. **inverse:** (of a proportion) containing quantities of which an increase in one results in a decrease in another. A quantity is said to be in inverse proportion to another quantity if it increases as the other decreases, or vice versa.

4

The Progress of a Message

4

The Progress of a Message

At the inception of a communications system in an organization, people will have to be constantly indoctrinated about the proper form of a message. That form should be simple and unvarying. Essential features are: origin point, destination, velocity, importance and origin time. These would all appear in a routine manner on the message, either in a line across the top, or in various boxes or customary placements on the page. These positions should have a recognized order, so that the whole thing can be rendered in a continuous stream, as on a teletype, without confusion or loss of data.

The communicator's task will be easier if the communication forms which are supplied have places clearly marked for each item of communications data. Some self-important individuals may feel that they do not need to fill in all these blanks. Some executives may balk[1] at the requirement of an *explanation* for every order. But the communicator will know that if an executive cannot put his order in the proper communication form, then that executive does not have a clear idea of what he is trying to do. That executive should think it over longer before trying

---

1. **balk:** stop, as at an obstacle, and refuse to proceed or to do something specified.

to communicate about it, because if he does not understand it himself, how will the receiver?

To make learning the form easy, the communicator should make up a sample message which contains all the possibilities and entries and distribute it to every office and desk. Copies of it should be posted in obvious locations. Individuals who have particular trouble might be presented with a copy to stand before them on the desk. Whenever the communicator receives a message which lacks some essential form or data, he should send it back to the originator until all messages are in proper form.

Some organizations may prefer to use the military system of twenty-four-hour designation, 0001 being one minute past midnight and 2400 being midnight.

The communicator will find that he or she is frequently having to grade communications down as to velocity. If the system is not overloaded, a traffic-velocity message would be delivered very quickly anyway, and the use of higher velocity grades on every message would result in slowing down the general flow by distracting the communicator from routine operations.

In Washington, during the 1941–46 war, messages which had to go fast were first graded as "Important." Then everything was marked "Important," since everyone felt important, and it became necessary to introduce a new grade, "Rush." After that, there was "Urgent," which was finally superseded by "Operational Priority." "Operational Priority" remained effective for some time, although it merely meant expedited handling. "Rush," by that time, had become the equivalent of "Slow Boat to China." A new designation was needed to speed really "important" messages on their way. One day, some pink slips appeared on boxes and envelopes, which were meant to fill the need. They bore the words "Super-Frantic-Hysterical!" Unless the communicator wishes to have to resort to means like this, he will have to be prepared to grade messages down regularly.

Another matter over which the communicator will have differences with the people he is serving might be labeled "rhetoric."[2] A message may try to get into the communication line which runs like this: "Jones to Smith—I would be very appreciative if you would kind of hang around the office on Thursday because—well, I have been looking over these chairs and desks that are in here, and they are in a terrible state of repair. Mr. Grapnel was saying to me, only the other day, that we have to present a businesslike appearance and look as though we were a prosperous firm. Well, there are three broken chairs right in this one office, and that doesn't look very prosperous to me. So, as I say, I called Mr. O'Reilly of the Seumas Furniture Company on the phone, and he says that he has to go out to Riverside on Wednesday and down to Richmond on Tuesday, and so he won't be able to get here until Thursday. Now, I know you have experience with furniture and know the costs and so forth, and so I would like it if you would be here when he comes so you can show him what is broken and arrange the whole thing with him. Thanks a lot.—Jones."

The communicator tells Mr. Jones that this message cannot get into the system the way it is written. For one thing, some of the data is missing. When is the appointment? For another thing, where is the record of the phone call? If Mr. O'Reilly comes and does some work or takes away some furniture on the strength of a phone call, the organization will have no memory of the transaction, and it may forget to pay Mr. O'Reilly or get the chairs back. Possibly a situation might arise whereby Mr. Jones might have to pay Mr. O'Reilly, since, according to memory, the

---

2. **rhetoric:** talk or writing that sounds grand or important but has little meaning.

transaction never took place. Third, the message is three times too long.

After Jones recasts[3] the message five more times, it will look something like this. "Jones to Smith—Would like you in room 101 at 2:30 P.M. Thursday (12 Feb.) to meet Mr. O'Reilly of the Seumas Furniture Company and arrange for his repair of three broken chairs and one desk (the small one). The preliminary arrangements with him are covered in the written record of the phone call, a copy of which is attached. Reason: The office looks shoddy, Mr. Grapnel has complained. You are the only one I know who knows anything about furniture except Hansen and he is on vacation. Thanks,—Jones." This would be a *very full* message, intended to get the best cooperation from Smith.

It is very easy to be erroneously brief as it is to be erroneously windy.[4] A system can be blown up by messages which are so brief that they seem angry or sarcastic.

Affinity,[5] *reality*[6] and *communication* make a triangle[7] which must be followed if the system is to be made to function well. Communication without affinity and without an effort to agree (reality) do not achieve their function of communicating. It is very easy for an originator to feel himself vastly important and commanding with a high-volume system at his command. It is

---

3. **recasts:** makes over; remodels.

4. **windy:** full of talk or verbiage (an excess of words beyond those needed to express concisely what is meant); talkative; long-winded.

5. **affinity:** degree of liking or affection or lack of it. Affinity is a tolerance of distance. A great affinity would be a tolerance of or liking of close proximity. A lack of affinity would be an intolerance of or dislike of close proximity. Affinity is one of the components of understanding. *See also* **ARC** in the glossary.

6. **reality:** the solid objects, the *real* things of life; the degree of agreement reached by two people. *See also* **ARC** in the glossary.

7. For further information on the affinity, reality and communication (ARC) triangle read *The Problems of Work* by L. Ron Hubbard.

---

easy for him to fall into the error of pounding the system to pieces with sharp, hammering messages. A system is like a mirror. He will get out of it about the same as he puts into it. Emotionally, then, the system has a certain tension. It is so responsive that it carries the exact emotion of the originator all the way through.

In old systemless businesses, an executive could snarl to his secretary to "Get that damned fool on the phone and tell him to . . ." The secretary knew enough to temper[8] the message. Indeed, she was expected to temper the message. If she had quoted her executive exactly, he, no doubt, would have had her fired or at least refused to take her to the "Kit-Kat"[9] that night.

A communicator for an executive is faced with the same problem. But originators often have no communicator tempering their snaps and snarls. The befuddlement[10] of old systemless businesses kept most of this entheta (snaps and snarls and bad data) from arriving with impact. But on a communications system, anything put into line comes out quickly at the other end. And it comes out with exactly the same emotion that it went in with. And it will very probably come back with the same emotional tone. A system, then, is capable of taking on the tone of its originators. Indeed, originators full of pomposity[11] and bad temper can blow themselves straight off the line. And shops which are mad at executives can, as originators, blow themselves rapidly into reorganization.

---

8. **temper:** to soften or tone down.

9. **''Kit-Kat'':** a made-up name for a nightclub, an establishment for evening entertainment, generally open until the early morning, that serves liquor and usually food and offers patrons music, comedy acts, a floor show or dancing; nightspot.

10. **befuddlement:** confusion; muddle.

11. **pomposity:** the quality of being pompous, characterized by an exaggerated display of self-importance or dignity; boastfulness; arrogance.

Irritated, harsh, commanding-without-reason messages break channels. This is a mechanical fact. And it is a very important fact for unless it is understood, the best communications system in the world, carrying the bad temper of a chief executive, will blow him apart on the backfire. He should remember, whatever originator is in a commanding position, that the entire area of his command, by the facility of this system, will be better acquainted with him and his habits and tempers than ever before. And because they can so easily react, they will react just as thoughtlessly as he reacted when he wrote rude or coarse messages. Messages should carry, wherever possible, a high, constructive tone.

The tone of the messages from the chief executives of a business or industry or government, when carried on a good system, will become the tone of the entire area. For the first time, a chief executive of a company can find his own constructive purposes understood and mirrored throughout his organization. But, on the other hand, a bad emotional state on the part of the chief executive can easily blow the entire area into chaos if he puts that emotion into the lines. If he wants to communicate, let him understand that he must also express affinity and reality, for none of these three will stand alone. It may be a temptation to write at the bottom of a confused message "Oh, my God!" and send it back to a subordinate as an acknowledgment. But, temptation yielded to, the subordinate ordinarily cannot restrain himself from reacting to this "Oh, my God!" on the comm lines.[12]

A high-placed originator can permeate an entire system with his mood. He can instill enthusiasm and loyalty and efficiency simply by the courtesy and temper of his despatches for

12. **comm lines:** (short for **communication lines**) the routes along which a communication travels from one person to another; the lines on which particles flow; any sequences through which a message of any character may go. *See also* **communication** in the glossary.

he is, after all, *cause*[13] in his area. It all depends on what he wants to cause. And he causes it with the tenor[14] of his despatches. If an executive does not care to believe the importance of this, let him send out, some morning, five sarcastic or bitter despatches and then check his plant; he will find that his sarcasm or bitterness did not stop with the people who received those despatches. It went straight on through to the machines themselves. Enough of it can cause actual mechanical breakdowns throughout the area, not for any mystic[15] reason but because the sergeant kicked the private and the private kicked the mule.

We have been talking about the communication line "to" a person or a department. This may have suggested a one-way flow. *But no communication line is open and working without a two-way flow.* To and from. It is this two-way flow which permits the communications system to perform its most important job: seeing that the messages do not die before they have been either complied with or openly refused. The mechanism which accomplishes this is called the "time machine."[16]

---

13. **cause:** the point of emanation (something coming forth from a source). It could be defined also for purposes of communication, as source-point. If you consider a river flowing to the sea, the place where it began would be the source-point or *cause,* and the place where it went into the sea would be the effect-point and the sea would be the effect of the river. The man firing the gun is cause; the man receiving the bullet is effect.

14. **tenor:** the course of thought or meaning that runs through something written or spoken.

15. **mystic:** of hidden meaning or nature; mysterious.

16. **time machine:** a series of baskets, one for each day of the week, used to keep track of an executive's orders and to report back to the executive either compliance or noncompliance with the order. A carbon copy of the order is placed in today's basket when it is received, and it is advanced one basket every morning. When compliance to the order is received, it is clipped to the order and sent to the issuing executive. If the order is not complied to within a week, it falls off the *time machine* by appearing in the basket being emptied on that day. The copy of the order is then returned to the issuing executive to show his order has not been complied with, so that he can handle the situation.

The very smallest number of copies which could exist of any communication would be two: one to go, one to stay until the other one came back. Why this? Because, if one stays until the other one comes back, the communicator, and through him the originator, will know whether or not this order has been complied with. The message cannot die secretly. So long as that second copy is sitting in the basket or hanging on the peg marked "uncompleted," the message is alive—somebody is going to do something if the first copy doesn't come back. If the second copy is not there, the first copy can get lost or be forgotten, and nothing will be done. Nothing can be done. The only person who can do anything is the originator. But the originator is on the command line, he is a planner. He is not supposed to be worrying about whether messages live or die. He has no time for that. He has planned and issued his order. From then on it should be automatic—either compliance or refusal. The communications system exists to free the planner from his worry, and the time machine is the means by which the job is done.

If there were any sign of poor communication on the part of some individual in the command line, the communicator using this communications system would begin sending nudges to this individual, requesting the completion of the communication. These nudges would all remain as a permanent part of the record of that communication, in the file.

An individual who failed to answer a nudge would normally blow right off the communication line after a very short time. In other words, the command function of the organization would be informed that there was a break in communication in the vicinity of this individual, and the command function would be asked to find out why. A vice-president would drop in on the individual to have a heart-to-heart talk. Naturally, the individual would not be there. He could not be there and fail to answer a nudge. It would be unthinkable not to answer a nudge, if he were there. So he would be absent. The communications system would have reported this absence, without even trying to, as a byproduct of keeping the communication lines open.

An organization in which all the communication lines are open and flowing is a healthy organization. There is no way to hide trouble with a fully open communications system in operation.

The acknowlegment of a message in an organization is the equivalent of the helmsman's[17] repeating of the orders he receives on a ship. The helmsman has to repeat his orders, because if he does not, the ship runs aground. Organizations do not run aground with a splintering crash, spewing debris all over the sea. But organizations do run aground, and for the very same reasons that ships do. They run aground because their communications fail to flow.

---

17. **helmsman:** the person who steers a ship.

5

Costs, Leaks and Reasons

5

Costs, Leaks and Reasons

One of the worst communications systems known to man is the US Navy letter system. Because messages travel wholly on the command line, they are hopelessly bogged down in command protocol.[1] It takes almost as long to write one of these letters as it would to chisel a good communication on the same subject in stone: "To . . . From . . . Subject . . . References . . . Enclosures . . . via . . . One, (the substance of the epistle[2]) . . . Two, . . . Three, . . . Four, . . . Signature . . . bar line at bottom . . . First endorsement (taking care of the first names of 'Via') . . . Second endorsement (second name) . . ." The first endorsement is written, "From . . . To . . . Subject . . . Signature . . ." So is the second. It is like sending an airmail letter from Los Angeles to New York which has to change planes

---

1. **protocol:** the code of ceremonial forms and courtesies, of precedence, etc., accepted as proper and correct in official dealings. For example, in the navy, there are certain courtesies which a junior officer observes in dealing with senior officers, including how to address senior officers, when to salute, when to remove the cap, etc. The standard form for a business letter or contract would also be an example of protocol.

2. **epistle:** a communication made to an absent person in writing; a letter. Chiefly (from its use in translations from Latin and Greek) applied to letters written in ancient times, especially to those which rank as literary productions, or to those of a public character or addressed to a body of persons. Used with a playful or sarcastic implication in application to ordinary (modern) letters.

---

at Phoenix, Albuquerque, Fort Worth, Dallas, Little Rock, Memphis, Nashville, Louisville, Cincinnati, Columbus, Pittsburgh, Harrisburg, Philadelphia and Newark. You could call this airmail if you wanted to; and the Navy can call its letter system communications.

Going back over the order books of Napoleon,[3] one may find little masterpieces of communication. Of course, Napoleon had no system such as the one we are describing. When he had spoken, he had spoken, and it was mostly up to luck from then on. There was no evaluation and no time machine to keep his order boiling[4] until it was complied with. No one was assigned to the regimental commander as communicator. If the regimental commander was in the habit of sending out "D5s," there was no way for Napoleon to find this out.

More battles are lost because of lack of communications than because of lack of strategy. The absence of back-flow has done more damage than the absence of brilliance. Many a brilliant planner has wasted his ideas by pouring them into a non-functional communication line. Nelson[5] knew about this. He partly solved the problem by calling all his captains in before an engagement and explaining his ideas to them. He told them what he was trying to accomplish and how he intended to accomplish it, and he let them work out their own way of fitting in with his very simple plan. This was good planning, but we mention it here because it minimized the amount of

3. **Napoleon:** Napoleon Bonaparte (1769–1821), French military leader and emperor of France (1804–15).

4. **boiling, keep (something):** keep anything going (from the agitated motion of boiling water); in this sense, ensuring that an order is not just dropped or forgotten, but is kept moving toward completion.

5. **Nelson:** Horatio Nelson (1758–1805), admiral in the English navy, known as one of the greatest of naval strategists.

communication which had to go on during the battle. Nelson solved his communications problem by eliminating much of the necessity for communications.

In the navies of the world, a fast communications system was evolved, the remarkable system known as "Flag-Hoist." Now it is backed up by blinkers using the same code as the flag-hoist.

A few decades ago, a fleet could operate in unison, carry out all necessary operations, convoy,[6] fight or flee, using nothing more than a few pieces of cotton hanging on a yardarm.[7] In the 1941–46 war, this system, with blinkers added, was used by ships to hunt submarine wolf packs.[8] Somewhat earlier, Genghis Khan[9] used a similar system for cavalry operations.

An example of the flag-hoist system is this. The flag representing T (called "tare") goes up the flag hoist along with a flag representing 9. This means "Turn ninety degrees to the right." If 9 is above T, however, it means "Turn ninety degrees to the left." The flagship runs this signal up. All the other ships do the same, in acknowledgment. The moment of execution comes as soon as all ships have acknowledged. At that moment, with all signalmen standing at alert, the flagship brings its flags down again, and the order is executed. All the ships turn simultaneously to the right, ninety degrees. A difference in flags can make the

6. **convoy:** accompany (a ship, fleet, supplies, etc.) in order to protect; escort.

7. **yardarm:** the outer portion of a yard. A *yard* is a large wooden or metal rod crossing the masts of a ship horizontally or diagonally, from which a sail is set. The *yardarms* are the end sections of the yard on either side of the ship.

8. **wolf packs:** groups of submarines operating together in hunting down and attacking enemy convoys.

9. **Genghis Khan:** (1162–1227) Mongol conqueror of most of Asia and of east Europe. He was known to be ruthless in war, but he built an empire which lasted until 1368.

order either "ninety degrees from compass course"[10] or "ninety degrees from relative course."[11] This system is one of the fastest in the world. The order to execute comes as fast as it could by radio. It is a good system. It keeps men alive in battle.

A principle of communication which the communicator must know is that a communication line is a good line in proportion to the abundance of theta and the paucity[12] of MEST which are on it. MEST is matter, energy, space and time. This means that a communications system should always look for ways to cut down the amount of material which has to be used to transmit a message; to find ways of accomplishing the task with a minimum of mechanical energy, both from machines and from human beings; to find the shortest routes through space; to use the least amount of time.

The first attempts to do this will involve, on the part of some, efforts to do away with the number of copies of a message. This will be the most obvious MEST in the system and these unfortunates will try to improve the system by cutting down the number of copies. This is quite similar to trying to cure a psychotic by disconnecting him from his brain by surgery. Cutting down the number of copies destroys the back-flow and destroys the memory. Cutting down the number of copies destroys the communications system and leaves no MEST for the theta to travel on. At this stage in man's development, his theta requires MEST to express itself. When the race achieves universal

---

10. **compass course:** a course whose bearing is relative to the meridian (one of the great circles of the Earth passing through the poles and any given point on the Earth's surface) as given by the navigator's compass, no compensation being made for variation or deviation.

11. **relative course:** angle between the course of one's own ship and that of another adjacent ship.

12. **paucity:** smallness of quantity; scarcity; scantiness.

ESP,[13] communications systems may no longer need any MEST at all. Now, they do.

The communicator is responsible for the memory of the organization. The biggest leak in the memory of the organization will be the executive who gets on the phone and talks for half an hour and does not make any record of what went on or permit any to be made. In a long telephone conversation between two planners, a communicator should be listening in on the line, making notes. It does no good to record the conversation mechanically—except for court evidence. No one has time to listen to recordings. Still, a record must be kept. If the material does not get into the communications system in written form, it will be as though the conversation never had taken place.

The executive may complain about making a record of the call himself. He may say that he hasn't time to do it. The communicator's answer is, "If you do not make a record of your agreement and commitment, nobody in the organization can follow through. You complain of being overworked. The reason you are overworked is that nobody in the organization can follow through on the things you initiate. It is not that people won't cooperate with you. It is just that they don't know what you want done. When you talk to Mr. Smith at the bank and he says he will lend you that $15,000 to put in the new arborvitae[14] on the front lawn, you must take the communication blank which is on your desk and write a confirmation message, giving all the

---

13. **ESP:** extrasensory perception: perception or communication outside of normal sensory capability, as in telepathy and clairvoyance (the supernatural power of seeing objects or actions removed in space or time from natural viewing).

14. **arborvitae:** any of several ornamental or timber-producing evergreen trees of the cypress family, native to North America and eastern Asia, having a scaly bark and scalelike leaves on branchlets.

data in the tersest[15] possible form. Sign it. Send it through the communications system. It will go to Mr. Smith at the bank, and he will confirm it by signing his copy. The organization will remember it. In short, it will have happened. If you do not do this, then it never happened. . . ."

Having his own communicator, the executive may balk at having his conversations listened to. The argument is still the same. The communicator does not care at all what the executive says on the telephone. He does not care how long the executive talks on the phone or to whom. His only attitude is: "If there is no record of this call to confirm it, then it never happened, and you have wasted your time."

Executives will get used to having communicators listening in on their calls. They will learn to appreciate the value of the communicator's insisting that the agreement which is reached be stated clearly and precisely for the record. It has to be written down. If no agreement is reached, the record should say so: "Talked to Jinks of Teamsters' Union for two hours, about contract. No agreement reached. Jinks got mad, and so did I. (Signed) Jones." This is a useful record. This could be sent to Jinks for confirmation, even. He would confirm it. He would be glad to. This sort of thing gives the organization a record of what has been going on. If somebody says, "Jones does no work all day long," the record is in the files to show what Jones did all day long. If there is a voice recording of the conversation, it can be filed with the confirmation report—but no one ever will play it; that is certain.

The wildest things can happen in the absence of such a system. A strange fellow turns up in the personnel office and

15. **tersest:** most neatly or effectively concise; briefest while retaining substance or meaning.

says, "I was talking to the administrator, and he hired me for $185 a day."

The personnel man thinks, "My God, that sounds like a lot of money for this guy, but maybe it's all right . . . I don't know. . . ." He tries to get in touch with the administrator.

"Sorry, Mr. Jones is gone for the day. He has a business conference out of town . . . won't be back till tomorrow morning." The personnel man hangs up.

The fellow says, "I'm supposed to paint some murals in the banquet hall. I'm supposed to get started right away, because he's giving a party Friday. . . ." The personnel man does not know what to do. He tears his hair.

When the executive is finally reached, at his home after the opera, at eleven o'clock at night, the personnel officer asks him, "Is this really on the level about Ziegschwillen?"

"Who is Ziegschwillen? And why are you bothering me at this hour of the night?"

"You know, the fellow you hired today to do the . . ."

"Have you been drinking, Smith?"

"No sir. This fellow came in and said you were giving him $185 a day . . ."

''What?''

"Yes, sir, to do the . . ."

"I never heard of Ziegschwillen! Throw him out!"

"Yes, sir."

The executive is out of town until Friday. Friday morning he shows up in the banquet hall and lets out a roar: "*Where are my murals?* What was the name of that painter, Sally?"

"Ziegschwillen, sir."

"Ziegschwillen? . . . *Ziegschwillen* . . . Somebody was *talking* to me about Ziegschwillen . . . Now let's see . . . Who was it? . . ."

Communications!

Management, planners worry about morale; they ought to worry about communication. Good communication is good morale. Bad communication is bad morale. Military organizations hire dancing girls, buy cola by the train load, buy baseball suits, install soda fountains, make church compulsory; in short, do almost anything to raise morale. They are trying, but they do not know what morale is. The only way to raise morale is by good, solid planning toward known goals, by providing food, clothing and shelter (even if portable), and by keeping the communication lines up.

Good communication makes it possible for all the people in an organization to do useful work every day instead of the administration's working forty-eight hours a day and everyone else's hanging around trying to find out what the administration wants them to do. People do not like to loaf. They do not like being off the communication line. It makes them feel that they are not really part of the operation. Management should realize that its ideas are vitally important to everyone in the organization—not so they can jump to attention, salute and begin to dig holes and fill them up, but so they can all be part of the operation, working together toward a known, common goal.

The communicator may use this fact in his effort to sell communications to backward executives. "The organization wants to know what you are thinking, Mr. Jones. The men down in the shop can't do their job without knowing. It raises morale all around, as well as preventing duplications and waste."

Or, the communicator may have this problem: "People aren't reading your orders carefully, Mr. Jones. They are too long and too numerous. The things you have to say are too important to the operation to be lost in wordiness and contradiction. We must make these orders easier for the plant to understand, so that your planning will not be wasted."

Or, this: "Your orders are not specific enough, Mr. Jones. You have so much of this information at your fingertips that you take it for granted everyone else has, too. But some of them have not been with us long, and most of them do not see the problem in the scope in which you see it. If you cannot make your orders more specific, they may be misinterpreted, and your planning may be wasted."

The communicator will find that management likes having its planning considered valuable, likes feeling that someone does not want it to be wasted. Management which feels that it is appreciated for its planning (not for its leniency or democratic-ness) will not feel the desire to be authoritarian. Almost anyone can follow a good plan. Not many men can make a plan which can be followed. When the communicator uses this approach, he is getting to the executive on a solid, theta line; he is using constructive reason.

Every order must have an explanation.

Military organizations have a law against explaining orders. It is not for a man to know why. It is for a man to do. However, men who do not know why, do not do—no matter how urgent the order is. To overcome this difficulty, the order is worded in threats: "Any man who goes off the ship on liberty before 1600 hours (4 P.M.) will be denied liberty for the next two weeks." Fine! This produces a large spirit of cooperation. And why was this order necessary in the first place? Because the preceding order said, "All men will go on liberty at 1600 hours," and there was no explanation given. The captain held liberty until that time because he wanted his ship loaded. A good reason. Why didn't he say so? How easy it would have been! "Liberty not granted until 1600. We want to get the ship loaded and ready for sea, so that we will have no worries tomorrow." Everyone would have said, "Good! Let's fix her up and then go ashore and have a good time." Instead of that, the petty officers are saying, "To hell with it!" There are two parts to an order: the directive, and the reason for the directive.

There is nothing wrong with an outright command, but it should be explained. There is nothing wrong with the commander's saying, "You men go up that hill and take it." That is not authoritarian, that is planning. But it is a poor commander who will not add, "This hill overlooks enemy artillery which is out-flanking our own artillery, making the advance impossible along all other points on the line." Maybe this information will fall into enemy hands and do a lot of damage, but it will do more damage if it is not issued. The hill may not be taken at all. It certainly will not be taken as well. "Why in hell are we taking this hill? It's just a hill."

6

Command Line and Comm Line

6

Command Line
and Comm Line

It is of great interest to the communicator to save the organization money. He can use this as a yardstick of the efficiency of his communications system. If he can save money by his system and within his system and still keep the communications flowing, he has a good system.

If telegrams are constantly traveling back and forth between two points, the communicator should look them over and find out what is happening. Is this much traffic necessary? Perhaps these people need to be indoctrinated in how to write a telegram. Does it take an exchange of six messages to convey information which could have been conveyed in two messages if they had been properly written? Of course, in an established communications system which was operating fully, these wires would be going through a communicator, who would not pass them unless they gave the obviously necessary data.

Some people will try to be too brief, and so will leave out data. Some will talk a lot but forget data. Some will leave data out on purpose—and what a good communications system will do to people like that will be a pleasure to see.

When communications begin to cost a lot of money, there must be something wrong with the organization. It is up to the communicator to see this and report it to the highest echelon. "This place must be in a mess, Mr. Jones. I have two lines here that won't work at all, and there is too much communication required for the amount of work that gets done."

The executive has an automatic check on the structure of his organization, and on the operation of the personnel within that structure. Suppose that instrument manufacture has been put under the command of body division because it happens to occupy space near the body division. There will be a constant stream of communication from the instrument section to the ignition department. When the body section executive communicates with the instrument section, however, his communication line will not operate properly, because the people in instruments resent his interference. This situation will show up in the communications office. If the chief executive wants to examine his organization, he should look to see where the lines are flowing too little and where they are glutted. This will tell him either that he should indoctrinate some individuals or that there is something inefficient about his command structure.

An executive has command power in an organization. Usually, his inefficiencies are tolerated in ratio to the amount of command power he has. But the altitude of an individual on the command line is also a measure of the effect that his acts and communications are going to have on the organization. Therefore, his idiosyncrasies[1] should be less tolerated, when it comes to communication.

If the janitor says that he thinks the organization is full of German spies, no one will pay any attention. But if the second vice-president says, "You know, we have to be very careful.

---

1. **idiosyncrasies:** characteristics, habits, mannerisms or the like that are peculiar to an individual.

Foreign agents are everywhere. I have my suspicions about various people right in this organization." What will happen? A tidal wave[2] of rumors; the whole plant in an uproar.

As a man rises higher and higher on the command line, he belongs more and more to the organization. When he reaches the top, he belongs to it twenty-four hours a day, seven days a week, fifty-two weeks a year and one more day on leap year. He is epitomizing[3] the life of the organization. The members of the organization can respect him for this only if he communicates well to them. If he does not, he might as well not be in command.

The chief executive must be the best trained, best disciplined, most thoroughly indoctrinated person in the organization, where communication is concerned. If he wants to come to work at noon and go home at midnight, if he wants to upholster his office in purple-dyed polar bear skin, if he wants to have seven singing secretaries, this is nobody's business but his own. But if he does not communicate well, this is everybody's business, and he should be indoctrinated in communication or turn his job over to a man who can learn communication.

The chief executive is particularly important to communication not only because he is the top of the command line, but because he has command over the communications system. If the chief executive understands what communication is and why the communication lines have to be separate and distinct from the command network, the system will function. If he does not, very soon the communications system will begin to mingle

---

2. **tidal wave:** any widespread or powerful movement, opinion or tendency; literally means a large destructive ocean wave produced by a seaquake (an earthquake on the ocean floor), hurricane or strong wind.

3. **epitomizing:** being representative or typical of the characteristics or general quality of a whole class.

with the command line, and at that moment the whole project can be junked.[4]

In the past, command charts have been thought to be communications charts. They aren't. Beautiful charts, in ten colors, sit all over the Defense Department, the Navy, the government, state capitols, county seats,[5] hospitals, etc. At the top, there is the president or the chief nurse or the Secretary of Defense, and from there run lines to all members and sections of the organization. The moment people in this organization get a look at this chart and decide that it is a communications chart, the organization is as good as dead. What the secretary tells the undersecretary is supposed to be told to the assistant, who will tell it to the general, who will tell it to the colonel, and so on down the line to the sergeant, who will do it. On a basis of command, this is true. But on a basis of communications, this is not true.

We would not take a planning machine, some device that was charting courses for 195 air flights simultaneously, and put a speaker on one side of it and a teletype on the other, and expect it to listen to the speaker and whenever the speaker said "Bingo" relay that information and type "Bingo" on the teletype. This would be an interruption of the planning machine. It would be using a 195-problem-capacity computer just to relay the word "Bingo." That would be silly. But that is what is done to administrators and executives.

Some executives who are entangled in these communication-command chimeras[6] do not realize how overloaded they

---

4. **junked:** cast aside as junk; discarded as no longer of use; scrapped.

5. **county seats:** towns or cities that are the centers of government of counties.

6. **chimeras:** often fantastic combinations of incongruous parts, especially those calculated to deceive. The term comes from the name of a monster, the *Chimera*, in Greek mythology which breathed fire and had a serpent's tail, a goat's body and a lion's head.

are by having to listen for "Bingo" and repeat "Bingo" forty times a day. They take it all in stride until one day the man on their left says "Bingo" and they, in their preoccupation, turn to the man on their right and say "Cheesecake." Two months later the head of the armament[7] division receives the message:

"Forty thousand cheesecakes have been purchased according to your order. What should we do with them?"

"*What* cheesecakes?"

The executive who let that one slip gets shipped out to the wide-open spaces, and he never knows what happened.

The commanding general tells his regimental commander. The regimental commander tells his adjutant.[8] They think this is communications. It is not. If an efficient organization chart is to be drawn up, it must have two parts: command and communication. They could be drawn on the same board, in two different colors. The hub of the command chart would be the chief executive, but the hub of the communications chart would be the central communications office.

A *communicator* exists wherever there is a command point of any volume of output. Where there is a general, there is a general's communicator. The communicator has to find out (from the general) what the general wants to do, what is his goal. Then he has to find out (through the communications system) where the troops are located and whether the horses have had fodder.[9]

---

7. **armament:** war equipment and supplies.

8. **adjutant:** an officer in the army whose business it is to assist the superior officers by receiving and communicating orders, conducting correspondence and the like.

9. **fodder:** coarse food for cattle, horses, sheep, etc., as cornstalks, hay and straw.

"General, sir. The horses have been without fodder for five days."

"What! I didn't know that."

If the general has a communicator he finds this out in time to make another plan. If he has no communicator, the cavalry charges a hundred yards and all the horses fall flat on their faces.

"They have been without fodder for five days, General."

"Why didn't somebody tell me?"

Somebody didn't tell him because he was in command. Command has the habit of assuming to itself pompous robes,[10] and so information does not flow up to it easily. If the information flows up to it at all it is usually from some highly manic[11] individual who charges in under a full head of steam[12] and spills a great load of entheta. An organization can be wrecked this way.

When the general has had to put up with a certain amount of this sort of thing, he goes crazy and makes a rule that all his orders are to be obeyed and that nobody is to ask why. This, then, produces a modern military organization.

A communications station should exist for every command post, or terminal. A shadow of this exists today in secretaries but

---

10. **pompous robes:** literally, apparel or dress characterized by a pretentious or conspicuous display of dignity or importance in an attempt to impress others. Used figuratively in this sense.

11. **manic:** excessively excited or enthusiastic; crazed.

12. **head of steam:** literally, the pressure exerted by confined fluid, used to generate mechanical power. Used figuratively in this sense to mean being very excited or angry about something.

they have no power to demand and produce good communications. They do the best they can, but they depend too much on the good will of the executive. If the executive hates to communicate, the secretary does not dare to communicate, for fear of losing her job.

In the army, the adjutant cannot be a good communicator because he is too dependent on the general. His promotion depends on whether or not he is cheerful and happy and can balance a cup of tea properly at parties.

The adjutant says to the general, "General, sir, the ammunition is sitting in ten feet of water."

The general jumps, then looks angry. "Well, don't tell them anything about that."

"But, General . . ."

"Major Bluddboil, you will oblige me by not arguing!"

"Yes, sir."

Communication. If the major tries this more than a few times, the general will send a letter to the department reqesting that the major be shipped out to the wide-open spaces because he is "always arguing." *This* message, by the way, will go right through, without a hitch.

7

Mail and the Littered Desk

7

Mail and the Littered Desk

One of the biggest jobs of any organization is mail. Some organizations have mail as ninety-five percent of their operation. Others just have a whopping[1] big number of letters to write. But people, for some reason, seem to take mail for granted: "Well, I haven't anything to do this afternoon. I guess I'll catch up on some of my mail." Mail is the first point at which any organization's communication breaks down.

An executive's desk is sometimes as clean as a new penny — but don't open the center drawer: there is a month's accumulation of letters in it! There is a good reason for this. The executive's time is being taken by many people and many problems. He keeps putting things off. He says he will make up his mind about it Tuesday. By Tuesday, he has forgotten about it, and it dies in his desk drawer. That center desk drawer of the executive is the bottleneck[2] in the organization.

An executive's desk should be as littered and confused as the operation is. If there are a lot of loose ends in the operation,

---

1. **whopping:** extremely, exceedingly.

2. **bottleneck:** any point at which movement or progress is slowed up because much must be funneled through it.

there should be a lot of loose pieces of paper on the executive's desk—one for each loose end. Or, there should be a communications system which will keep these things in plain sight until they are cared for.

Nothing should be filed until it is dead. If it is filed before it is dead, it dies in the file, and after a while the organization begins to develop a very unpleasant aroma.

If the organization is not confused at all, the last point of clearance should be the executive's desk. The beautiful, clean desk is just a myth. "Grapnel is so efficient! His desk never has anything on it at all." This statement presents two possibilities: either it is false or it is true. If it is true, it represents an organization without flaw.

An executive should not have to answer mail if he does not want to. Mail is a function of the mail section. If a letter comes asking for employment, the executive may care to read it, but he may not care to answer it. Under normal circumstances, if he has no secretary, this will mean that the letter does not get answered—which is bad public relations for the organization. There may be a big, expensive public relations department trying to build up affinity with the public, but the real public relations of this company consist of business relations. So the letter should be answered. A mail section would answer this letter. The executive would write "Answer: insufficient experience, no position open. Jones." The mail section would write a letter. Mail would not pile up on Jones' desk.

On the other hand, if Jones likes and has time to answer his own letters, he should not be allowed to monopolize[3] the time of the communications system by calling a girl into his office every

_____

3. **monopolize:** obtain exclusive possession of, keep entirely to oneself.

half hour to take dictation, while he hems and haws.[4] He should do his hemming and hawing into a dictating machine, if he cannot face a typewriter.

Let us imagine an organization in which there are a hundred command points at which letters are likely to be written to the public, but only twenty of these are important enough to have their own communicators. For the other eighty, there might be a traveling dictation machine service as well as a quiet room for dictating. All the letters dictated but untyped in one day would be taken by the mail battery,[5] and letters would be typed first thing in the morning. There might be many ways of arranging this, to suit different organizations. The objective would be to have all letters going through the system with the least amount of effort on the part of the system and of the command points.

Ideally, mail would be handled like this:

A letter arriving in the mail, addressed to Jones, would be opened by the mail section (unless it was marked "Personal"). It would be read by a communicator (not a clerk) assigned to the mail section, and an office communication form would be written up containing the substance of this letter. This form, accompanied by the letter itself, then would go through the system to Jones, as a communication from the mail section to Jones. Jones would have to act, of course, because the time machine would be watching the progress of this communication. Note that the letter is not the communication: the letter is only "exhibit A," which goes along with the communication for reference. When Jones decides what he wants to do about the letter, he completes the

---

4. **hems and haws:** makes sounds as if one is clearing the throat, or gropes around in speech, while searching for the right words.

5. **battery:** a group of similar things arranged, connected or used together; set or series; array. Also refers to the personnel who operate such equipment.

8

Developing an Organization's Brain

It is the communicator's responsibility to handle in the best possible way all communications. Therefore, it is his responsibility to keep himself informed about existing communications facilities, to use the best equipment and methods, and to keep his staff informed about these things. (Heretofore, knowledge and operation of equipment has been considered the *only* job of a communicator.)

The communicator will know all the tricks for fast, volume communication at low cost. It may be that an organization has a moderate volume of high-velocity information every day between Los Angeles and New York. It would be up to the communicator to find the best way to transmit this.

It is possible, through a communications system, to organize files so that they are action files, so that they are the memory of a mind which thinks. A file should have three sections: (1) the action file, which holds a datum that calls for action at a certain time and injects it back into the system at the proper moment; (2) working files, which hold the information that is valuable to the operation; (3) dead files, which could be junked without any loss of value to the operation.

The action file would *not* be housed in a closed filing

cabinet. It would be out in plain sight, working all the time. Such a file can be visualized as an expanse of colored tabs with communications, hanging in racks. It also can be visualized as a battery of file machines and action card indexes. Whatever its form, it is alive with activity at all times.

The working file must be organized so that the information in it is available in association with related material, like the data in a mind. If it is not so organized, then it has no information in it, no matter how many facts are written down on pieces of paper in filing cabinets. The information should be organized, indexed, cross-indexed and activated so that when a communication comes through the system, a quick review of the related data can be made, as in a mind.

The navy file system is beautifully organized, but it does not tell anything. It is a filing system only, not a brain. Action and working files are a brain, which hold the memory of an organization. Closed file drawers, unorganized and unindexed, contain not memory, but library facts. They are useful only to the scholar.

A communications system is a reason system. It produces reason on an organizational level, just as the individual minds of the personnel produce reason on an individual level.

A CIC (Combat Information Center) could be organized, using the communications system, which would take care of the planning of an organization. A project would be initiated by management, and the brain of this organization would go into action to supply management with all the facts about the problem, arranged and related to present the best way of proceeding. Management would have to supply the direction of the operation, to supply the motivation. If the organization had good action and working files, decisions on problems that would arise would be almost automatic. How convenient for management to be thus freed to devote itself to *creative* planning—to letting the organization solve its own problems, while management looks around for new problems to solve, new fields to conquer!

The commander of a fleet does not have to supervise the aiming of guns. The CICs do that. They find the enemy, aim the guns and pick up the survivors. The CIC can perform any operation which has been performed once, or which is similar to one that has been performed once. This frees the commander to think up operations which never have been performed. This is what keeps the enemy off balance.

Management has a hard time in big industry because of the lack of an organizational brain to do the routine planning. One can imagine the industry of the future, in which management devotes many hours to an examination of goals and plans and a minimum to administration, in which management is able to be less a lion tamer and more an architect.

The communications system should put out a regular bulletin on the operation. A summary of each week's activities should be made from the time file.[1] Summaries of activities in various departments and along various lines should be made from the departmental files and from the subject file. All information that goes into files should be summarized in two or three separate reports. Then these reports should be further summarized into an operational bulletin for all to read. The purpose of this is the development of a brain in which any fact can be found and in which all facts which pertain to a given order will come up for examination automatically and in whatever detail the planner or communicator desires.

---

1. **time file:** a chronological file containing copies of the communications which have passed through the communications system and have been answered or complied with.

The construction of a brain is different from the construction of a computing machine. A computing machine has a limited language into which everything must be painfully translated. A brain must be able to perceive and remember and associate data universally, without special preparation of data. This means that the real work must be done by human minds, which are thought processes. The brain is only the channel through which all this thought operates.

9

Group Goals and Management

9

Group Goals and Management

**From an Essay by
L. Ron Hubbard**

It is an old and possibly true tenet of business—at least where business has been successful—that management is a specialty. Certainly it is true that ruling is a specialized art and craft not less technical than the running of complex machinery and certainly, until Scientology, more complex.

With our present technology about groups, it is possible to accomplish with certainty many things which, before, came out of guesses when they emerged at all. Management in the past has been as uncodified in its techniques as psychiatry, and management, with reservation, has almost always been a complete failure. Men were prone to measure the excellence of management in how many dollars a company accumulated or how much territory a country acquired. These are, at best, crude rules of thumb. Until there was another and better measure, they had to serve. To understand that these are not good measures of the excellence of management one has only to review the history of farms, companies and nations to discover that few have had any long duration and almost all of them have had considerable trouble. Management has failed if only because the "art" of managing, as practiced in the past, required too much hard labor on the part of the manager.

Until one has considered the definitions of wealth and expanded territory, and has taken a proper view on what these things really comprise, one is not likely to be able to appreciate very much about management, its problems or its goals. Hershey,[1] a brilliant manager with a brilliant managing staff, yet failed dismally as a manager because he neglected the primary wealth of his company—his people and their own pride and independence. His reign of a company ceased with his people— well-paid engineers and laborers, well housed, well clothed— shooting at him with remarkably live ammunition. The brilliant management of Germany came within an inch of restoring to her all her conquests of former years, yet laid Germany in ruins.

Before one can judge management one has to consider the goals of an enterprise and discover how nearly a certain management of a certain enterprise was able to attain those goals. And if the goal of the company is said to have been wealth, then one had better have an understanding of wealth itself, and if the goal is said to have been territory, then one had better consider what, exactly, is the ownership of territory.

Goals and their proper definition are important because they are inherent in the definition of management itself. Management could be said to be the planning of means to attain goals and their assignation for execution to staff, and the proper coordination of activities within the group to attain maximal efficiency with minimal effort to attain determined goals.

Management itself does not ordinarily include the discovery and delineation of the goals of a group. Management concerns itself with the accomplishment of goals otherwise determined. In

---

1. **Hershey, Milton:** (1857–1945), American industrialist, founder of a large chocolate-manufacturing business.

large companies the goals of the group are normally set forth by boards of directors. When this is done, the goals are assigned the nebulous word *policy*. In governments, goals, when they are assigned at all, generally stem from less formal sources.

Nations are so large that until they embark[2] upon conquests they usually have few national goals which embrace all the group. The government personnel itself has the goal of protecting itself and exerting itself in management, and the remainder of the group bumbles along on small subgoals. When a goal embracing a whole nation is advanced and defined, the nation itself coalesces[3] as a group and flashes forward to the attainment of advances. It is an uncommon occurrence at best that a nation has a goal large enough to embrace the entire group, thus governments are normally very poor, being management with only the purpose of managing. Asia Minor, given a goal by Mohammed,[4] exploded into Europe. Europe, given a goal by certain religious men to the effect that the city of the Cross[5] had better be attained, exploded into Asia Minor. Russia, selling five-year plans and world conquest plans and minority freedom plans, can have a conquest over any other nation without any large group goals. A good goal can be attained by poor management. The best management in the world never attained group support in toto[6] in the absence of a goal or in the embracing of a poor one. Thus Russia could be very badly managed and succeed better than an excellently managed but goalless United

2. **embark:** set out on a venture; commence.

3. **coalesces:** unites or comes together, so as to form one.

4. **Mohammed:** (A.D. 570–632) Arab prophet, founder of Islam, the prominent religion of Asia.

5. **Cross, city of the:** the city of Jerusalem, where per the Bible, Jesus Christ was crucified on the cross.

6. **in toto:** as a whole; in its entirety; totally; altogether.

States (for self-protection is not a goal, it's a defense). Marx[7] is more newly dead than Paine.[8] The goal is less decayed.

Companies obtain, usually, their "policy" from an owner or owners who wish to have personal profit and power. Thus a sort of goal is postulated.[9] Nations obtain their goals from such highly remarkable sources as a jailbird[10] with a dream of a conquered enemy or a messiah[11] with cross in hand and Valhalla[12] in the offing.[13] National goals are not the result of the thinking of presidents or the arguments of assemblies. Goals for companies or governments are usually a dream, dreamed first by one man, then embraced by a few and finally held up as the guidon[14] of the many. Management puts such a goal into effect, provides the ways and means, the coordination and the execution of acts leading toward that goal. Mohammed sat alongside the caravan[15] routes until he had a goal formulated and then his followers managed Mohammedanism into a conquest of a large part of

---

7. **Marx:** Karl Marx (1818–83), German political philosopher, regarded by some as founder of modern socialism. The work he is most known for is *The Communist Manifesto*, in which he states that the evils of capitalist society cannot be abolished by reform but only by the destruction of the whole capitalist economy and establishment of a new classless society.

8. **Paine, Thomas:** (1737–1809) political philosopher and author. Paine emigrated to America from England in 1774. In 1776 he published a pamphlet (*Common Sense*) urging immediate declaration of independence, which had wide circulation and great influence in concentrating sentiment in favor of immediate independence.

9. **postulated:** put forward as a reality.

10. **jailbird:** a person who is or has been confined in jail; convict or ex-convict.

11. **messiah:** an expected liberator or savior of an oppressed people or country.

12. **Valhalla:** (*mythology*) the great hall where the god Odin receives and feasts the souls of heroes fallen bravely in battle. The word literally means *hall of the slain*.

13. **offing, in the:** in the projected future; likely to happen.

14. **guidon:** the identification flag of a military unit. Used figuratively.

15. **caravan:** of a group of travelers, as merchants or pilgrims, journeying together for safety in passing through deserts, hostile territory, etc.

civilization. Jefferson,[16] codifying the material of Paine and others, dreamed a goal which became our United States. An inventor dreams of a new toy, and management, on the goal of spreading that toy and making money, manages. Christ gave a goal to men. St. Paul[17] managed that goal into a group goal.

In greater or lesser echelons of groups, whether it is a marine company assigned the goal of taking Hill X428 by the planner of the campaign, or Alexander[18] dreaming of world conquest and a Macedonian[19] army managing it into actuality, or Standard Oil[20] girdling[21] the world because Rockefeller[22] wanted to get rich, the goal is dreamed by a planning individual or echelon and managed into being by a group. The dreamer, the planner, is seldom an actual member of the group. Usually he is martyred[23] to a cause, overrun and overreached. Often he lives to

---

16. **Jefferson:** Thomas Jefferson (1743–1826), third president of the United States. Jefferson wrote and presented the first draft of the Declaration of Independence in 1776.

17. **St. Paul:** (ca A.D. 3–68) Originally Saul, whose conversion to Christianity was attended by a vision. He became an apostle to the Gentiles, making several missionary journeys and founding many churches to which he sent letters which are now part of the New Testament. St. Paul was one of the greatest moral and spiritual teachers of his time.

18. **Alexander:** Alexander the Great (356–23 B.C.), king of Macedonia, an ancient kingdom located in what is now Greece and Yugoslavia.

19. **Macedonian:** of or having to do with Macedonia, an ancient country in the Balkan Peninsula, north of ancient Greece.

20. **Standard Oil:** an oil company incorporated by John D. Rockefeller in 1870 which grew very rapidly, becoming one of the largest oil companies in the United States at the time.

21. **girdling:** encompassing, enclosing, encircling.

22. **Rockefeller:** John Davison Rockefeller (1839–1937), American oil magnate; at one time was the world's richest man.

23. **martyred:** made into a martyr (a person who is put to death or endures great suffering on behalf of any belief, principle or cause).

bask[24] in glory. But he is seldom active management itself. When he becomes management, he ceases to formulate steps to be taken as lesser goals to greater goals and the group loses sight of its goal and falters. It is not a question of whether the dreamer is or is not a good manager. He may be a brilliant manager and he may be an utter flop. But the moment he starts managing, the group loses a figurehead[25] and a guidon and gains a manager.

The dreamer of dreams and the user of flogs on lazy backs cannot be encompassed in the same man, for the dream to be effective must be revered, and the judge and the taskmaster can only be respected. Part of a goal is its glamour and part of any dream is the man who dreamed it. Democracy probably failed when Jefferson took office as president, not because Jefferson was a bad president, but because Jefferson, engrossed[26] with management, ceased his appointed task of polishing up the goals.

According to an expert on history, no group ever attains a higher level of ideal or ethic than at the moment it is first organized. This observation should be limited, to be true, to those groups wherein management has been assigned to the dreamer of the dream. For in those cases where the dream was ably supported, the tone of the group remained high and the group continued to be brilliantly effective, as in the case of Alexander whose generals did all the generaling and Alexander, a brilliant individual cavalryman, set examples and pointed out empires.

---

24. **bask:** lie in or expose oneself to a pleasant warmth or atmosphere; used figuratively meaning to take pleasure or enjoyment (in).

25. **figurehead:** a person who is head of a group, company, etc., in title and is a symbol of the goals of that group.

26. **engrossed:** occupied completely, as the mind or attention, absorbed.

But whether a group has an Alexander or a wild-eyed poet or an inventor doing its goal setting for it, the group cannot be an actual or even an effective group without such goals for its achievement and without management brilliant enough to achieve those goals.

Having examined the source of such goals, one should also examine the character of goals in general. There are probably as many goals as there are men to dream them, probably more. Goals can be divided into two categories, roughly. The first would be survival goals and the second would be nonsurvival goals. Actually most goals are a combination of both, for goals are occasionally set forth solely for their appeal value, not for their actual value. One sees that the goal of a nation which directs it to conquer all other nations ends up, after occasional spurts of prosperity, in racial disaster. Such a goal is not dissimilar to the money goal of most "successful" industrialists or boards. One might call such goals acquisitive goals, entailing, almost exclusively, the ownership of the MEST accumulated through hard work by others. Technically one could call these enMEST[27] goals, for conquest of nations brings about the ownership of MEST which, by conquest, has been enturbulated[28] into enMEST and which will make enMEST of the conqueror's own land eventually. Rapacious[29] money gathering gains enMEST, not MEST, and makes enMEST of the rightful money of the acquisitor. Such goals, since they tend toward death, are then nonsurvival goals. Survival goals are good and successful in ratio to the amount of actual theta contained in them, which is to say, the ability of the goals to answer up favorably on a maximum number of

---

27. **enMEST:** MEST which has been confused and enturbulated, and thereby rendered less usable. *See also* **enturbulated** and MEST in the glossary.

28. **enturbulated:** made turbulent or agitated and disturbed.

29. **rapacious:** grasping; greedy.

dynamics.[30] A survival goal, then, is actually only an optimum solution to existing problems, plus theta enough in the dreamer to reach well beyond the casual solution. A group best catalyzes[31] on theta goals, not only to a higher pitch[32] but to a more lasting pitch than a group catalyzed by enMEST goals as in a war. It can be postulated that theta goals could bring about a much higher level of enthusiasm and vigor than the most grandly brass-banded[33] war ever adventured upon.

Another postulate is that a goal is as desirable as it contains truth or true advantage along the dynamics.

A group, then, can be seen to have three spheres of interest and action. The first is the postulation of goals. The second is management. The third is the group itself, the executors of the plans, procurers of the means and enjoyers of the victories.

These three factors or divisions must be satisfied to have a successful group or, actually, a true group. The divisions are not particularly sharp. The desires and thoughts of the body of the group influence and catalyze and are actually part of the goal dreamer. Management has to have the support of the group and the provision of the group to proceed at all and thus must have the agreement of the group for the best and most economical

---

30. **dynamics:** there could be said to be eight urges (drives, impulses) in life, which we call *dynamics*. They are motives or motivations. We call them the eight dynamics. These are urges for survival as or through (1) self, (2) sex and family, (3) groups, (4) all mankind, (5) living things (plants and animals), (6) the material universe, (7) spirits, and (8) infinity or the Supreme Being. For more information on the dynamics, see the book *Scientology: The Fundamentals of Thought* by L. Ron Hubbard.

31. **catalyzes:** changes, brings about or hastens a result, due to the stimulus of another thing or person.

32. **pitch:** comparative height or intensity of any quality or attribute; point or position on an ideal scale; degree, elevation, stage, status, level.

33. **brass-banded:** loudly and resoundingly promoted, as with bands (such as military bands) made up of brass and percussion instruments.

execution of orders. Management must have the confidence of the planning echelon or the planning echelon is liable to include the reform of management as part of the dream. The goal maker must be accepted and trusted by management or management will begin to look around for a new goal maker and, being management, not a goal maker, may take up with some highly specious[34] ideas which management might then seek to make a subechelon to itself (the thing which causes most nations to cave in and most companies to collapse).

There are three divisions of action, then, which are interactive and interdependent. ARC[35] amongst these three must be very high. A group which is hated by its management (often the case in the military) often gets wiped out; a whole system may be destroyed (as in American industry) when management and the group decide to become two camps. The death of the goal maker is not destructive to a group but even sometimes aids it, but only so long as the dream itself lives and is kept living. A management, for instance, which would interpose (for the "good" of the group) between the goal maker and the group is leveling death at the group by perverting and interpreting the character of the goal. Management cannot concern itself with the overall goal or plan; it can only execute and expedite the plans of accomplishing the goal and relegate its own planning to ways and means planning, not goal planning. The traffic between the group and the goal maker should be direct and clean of all

---

34. **specious:** having a fair or attractive appearance or character, calculated to make a favorable impression on the mind, but in reality devoid of the qualities apparently possessed.

35. **ARC:** a word made from the initial letters of *Affinity, Reality* and *Communication* which together equate to understanding. These are the three things necessary to the understanding of something—one has to have some affinity for it, it has to be real to him to some degree and he needs some communication with it before he can understand it. *See also* **affinity, reality** and **communication** in the glossary. For more information on ARC, read the book *The Problems of Work* by L. Ron Hubbard.

"interpretations" unless management wishes to destroy the group—in which case it should, by all means, undertake an interruption of communication between the goal maker and the group. The place of the goal maker is in the marketplace with the group or off somewhere sitting down thinking up a new idea. The place of management is in the halls and palaces, arsenals[36] and timekeepers' cages, behind the judges' bench and in the dispatcher's tower. Management leads the charge after goals has assigned the cause of the campaign.

Management is subservient to goals but goal making is not in command of management. So long as a management realizes this it will continue in a healthy state as a management, and the group, modified by natural factors such as food, clothing and general abundance, will remain in excellent condition. When management fails to realize this, the goal maker, even when he is merely an individual who enjoys the making of vast fortunes, shifts the management. When the goal maker is actually high theta and management forgets this and forgets the quality of ideas (or doesn't ever quite realize their potency) then, again and more so, management will be tumbled around, for a theta goal maker has behind him a group and in a moment can become much more group than management and easily empties out the halls and palaces. A management that discredits its goal maker or perverts the communication of goals of course dies itself but, in dying, may also kill a group.

Management often takes the goal maker into its confidence and requests the solution to various problems. Management should understand that when it does such a thing it is not taking conference with more management, for the advice it will receive on technical problems, no matter how brilliant, is usually

---

36. **arsenals:** government establishments where military equipment or munitions are manufactured.

delivered with asperity,[37] for the goal maker has no sight of tenuous lines of supply, quivering bank balances, raging labor leaders, leases and contracts unsigned or perilously inadequate. The goal maker sees goals, management sees obstacles to goals and ways of overcoming them. The first requisite of a goal maker is to see goals which are attainable only by the most violent ardures[38] and which are yet sparkling and alluring enough to lead forward and onward his own interest (in the case of an enMEST goal maker) or (if he is a theta goal maker) his entire group. Management pants between the pressure of the group to attain the goal and the clarion call[39] of the goal maker to go forward.

Yet there are specific means by which management can lighten the burdens for itself, recover and retain its own breath and be highly successful as management, which means that the group, by that management, must be highly successful if *its goals are kept bright*.

Let us concern ourselves only with true groups. The true group could be defined as one which has (a) a theta goal, (b) an active and skilled management working only in the service of the group to accomplish the theta goal, and (c) participant members who fully contribute to the group and its goals and who are contributed to by the group; and which has high ARC between goal and management, management and group, group and goal. Here we have no management problems beyond those natural problems of laying the secondary but more complex plans of

---

37. **asperity:** harshness or sharpness of tone, temper, or manner; severity.

38. **ardures:** a coined word meaning strong efforts; hard work to accomplish or achieve. Formed from the word *arduous*, derived from Latin *ardu-us*, which means "high, steep, difficult."

39. **clarion call:** a loud and clear call or summons; a ringing speech, phrase, etc., that stirs to action. A *clarion* is a shrill-sounding trumpet with a narrow tube, formerly much used as a signal in war.

accomplishing the goals, pointing out and laying the plans for the avoidance of obstacles en route to that goal or those goals and coordinating the execution of such secondary, but most vitally important, plans. Management, having the agreement of the participants, is immediately relieved by the participants of some of the planning and, that plague of management, the tying of loose and overlooked ends. Further, management is not burdened with the actual location or cultivation of food, clothing and shelter for the group as in a welfare state, but is only concerned with coordinating group location and cultivation. Management is enriched by the advice of those most intimately concerned with the problems of participation and is apprised[40] instantly of unworkabilities it may postulate. On the goal side it is relieved of the problem management has never solved, the postulation and theta-izing of the primary goals of the group. Further, management does not have the nerve-racking task of smoothing out enturbulations and confusions which are the bane[41] of every semigroup.

Now let us consider what might be meant by a true group as opposed to a pseudogroup. A true group falls away from being a true group in the gradient that ARC breaks[42] exist between goals and management, management and group, and group and goals. In the case of a high-theta goal maker and a group in agreement with those goals, a bond between group and goal maker is so copper-bound, cast-iron strong, whether the

---

40. **apprised:** given notice; informed; advised.

41. **bane:** cause of death, ruin or harm; curse.

42. **ARC breaks:** sudden drops or cuttings of a person's affinity, reality or communication with someone or something. Upsets with people or things (ARC breaks) come about because of a lessening or sundering (breaking apart) of affinity, reality, or communication or understanding. It is called an ARC break instead of an upset, because if one discovers which of the three points of understanding have been cut, one can bring about a rapid recovery in the person's state of mind. *See also* **ARC** in the glossary.

goal maker is alive or dead as a person, that a management out of ARC with either the goal maker or the group will perish and be replaced swiftly. But in the interim, while that management still exists, the group is not a true group and is not attaining its objectives as it should. This would be the first grade down from a true group toward a pseudogroup. The condition might obtain[43] for some time if management were not quite a true management and not flagrantly out of ARC. The duration that such a management would last would be inversely proportional to the completeness of the ARC break. A severe perversion or break of ARC would bring about immediate management demise. A continuing slight one might find the management tolerated for a longer time. The break with the group, while the goal maker lives, can be of greater severity than with the goal maker without causing management to collapse or be shifted. Break of ARC with a goal maker finds management under the immediate bombardment of a group catalyzed, as a small subgoal, into the overthrow of management. For this reason most managements prefer a good, safely dead goal maker whose ideals and rationale are solidly held by the group, and most groups prefer live goal makers because so long as the goal maker lives (in the case of a true group), the group has a solid champion, for a theta goal maker is mainly interested in the group and its individuals and his goals and has very little thought of management beyond its efficiency in accomplishing goals with minimal turmoil and maximal speed.

The next step down from the true group toward a pseudogroup is that point reached where the goals exist as codes after the death or cessation of activity, as a goal maker, of the goal maker. Management, always ready to assume emergencies exist, being hard-driven men even in the best group, breaks ARC to some slight degree with the codified goals in the name of

---

43. **obtain:** be prevalent, customary, or in vogue; prevail.

expediency. Being interested in current problems and seeing the next hill rather than the next planet, management innocently begins a series of such breaks or perversions and begins to use various means to sell these to the group. The group may resist ordinarily but in a moment of real danger may deliver to management the right to alter or suspend some of the code. If management does not restore the break with or perversion of the code, the true group has slipped well on its road to a pseudo-group.

The next major point on the decline is that point where management is management for the sake of managing for its own good, not according to the demised goal maker's codes of goals, but preserving only some tawdry[44] shadow of these such as "patriotism," "your king," "the American way," "every peasant his own landlord," etc.

The next step down is the complete break and reversal of ARC from group to management, at which moment arrives the revolution, the labor strikes and other matters.

If management succeeds the overthrown management without the simultaneous appearance of a new goal maker, the old regime, despite the blood let, is only replaced by the new one, for management, despite critics, is normally sincere in its efforts to manage, and strong management, unless a good theta goal maker springs up and carries through the revolution or strike, is faced with a continuing and continual emergency which demands the most fantastic skill and address on the part of managers and, oddly enough but predictably, the strongest possible control of the group.

We are examining here, if you have not noticed, the Tone

---

44. **tawdry:** of the nature of cheap finery; showy or gaudy without real value.

Scale of governments or companies or groups in general from the high theta of a near cooperative state, down through the 3^{45} of a democratic republic, down through "emergency management," down through totalitarianism, down through tyranny and down, if not resurged by a new goal maker somewhere on the route, into the apathy of a dying organization or nation.

A true group will conquer the most MEST. Not even given proportionate resources with another group, it will conquer other groups which are not quite true groups. Brilliance and skill tend naturally to rally to the standards of a true group as well as resources. As a sort of inevitable consequence, MEST will move under a true group. The amount of MEST a true group will eventually conquer—but not necessarily *own*—is directly in proportion to the amount of theta that group displays, theta being many things including solutions along the dynamics toward survival. To display theta the group must definitely tend toward a true group.

A truly successful management is a management in a true group. It is definitely in the interest of management to have as nearly true a group as it can possibly achieve. Indeed, management can actually go looking, for a group's completion, for a goal maker, or send the group looking for a goal maker and then, the goal maker proving himself by catalyzing the group's thoughts and ambitions, raise the goal maker's sphere of action as high as possible and abide thereby without further attempting to modulate or control the goals made (for management is necessarily a trifle conservative, is always liable to authoritarianism and is apt to be somewhat sticky of its power). Probably the most stupid thing a management can do is refuse to let a group become a true group. The group, if at all alive as individuals, will seek (the

---

45. **3:** the level 3.0 on the Tone Scale, conservatism. *See also* **Tone Scale** in the glossary, and the Tone Scale included in the Appendix, page 133.

third dynamic[46] being what it is) to become a group in the true sense. A group will always have around it a goal maker. Management in industrial America and in Russia tries to outlaw, fight and condemn goal makers. This places the group in the command, not of management, but of a would-be martyr, a John L. Lewis,[47] a Petrillo,[48] a Townsend,[49] and management promptly has to go authoritarian and start killing sections of the third dynamic—which course leads to death not only of the management but of the business or the nation.

Likewise a group should be tremendously aware of the dullness or the real danger of putting a goal maker into management or insisting that the goal maker manage. Hitler had a battle.[50] He probably had a lot of other battles he could have

---

46. **third dynamic:** the urge toward survival through a group of individuals or as a group. Any group or part of an entire class could be considered to be a part of the third dynamic. The school, the club, the team, the town, the nation are examples of groups. *See also* **dynamics** in the glossary.

47. **John L. Lewis:** (1880–1969) powerful labor leader in the United States from 1917 to 1940. Formerly president of the United Mine Workers, a labor movement to improve conditions for mine workers. Throughout World War II Lewis repeatedly called his miners out on strike, defying the government in many instances. In December 1946 a Federal court injunction was issued against the United Mine Workers, enjoining them to stop striking and levying fines of $3,500,000 against the group and $10,000 against Lewis personally.

48. **Petrillo:** James Caesar Petrillo (1892–1984), president of the American Federation of Musicians from 1940 to 1958. Petrillo organized several strikes—often without the support of public opinion—against radio, television and recording companies in order to strengthen the organization of his union and to combat increased use of technological devices which created less employment for musicians.

49. **Townsend:** Francis Townsend (1867–1960), American physician who originated legislation in 1934 to provide old-age pensions (Townsend plan) in the United States. Although bills to enact the Townsend plan were continually defeated, its popularity contributed to passage of Social Security legislation.

50. This refers to *Mein Kampf* (German, "My Battle"), an autobiographical account of Hitler's years of struggle against the government of Germany, and a statement of his program for restoring Germany to world power. It was written when Hitler was in prison in 1924. —Editor

---

written about if one and all had recognized what goal maker there was in him and supported his goal making. Instead, current management threw him into jail and sorted itself out as a target for national wrath (for don't think the people weren't behind Hitler, regardless of what the Nazis try to tell our military government). Down went the Republic,[51] up went Hitler as management. Down went Germany in a bath of blood. At best he was a bad goal maker because he dealt with enMEST, and very little theta. But he was a hideously bad manager, for by becoming one he could no longer be a good goal maker but, made irascible[52] by the confusions of management, went mad dog.[53]

Being rather low on the Tone Scale initially, most managements would be very chary[54] of creative-imagination-level goal making unless they knew the mechanics of the matter. And these demonstrate that it is unsafe to be without a goal maker, unsafe to suppress goal makers, unsafe not to keep trying for a true group continually, and unsafe not to fight very shy of letting anything drift toward the pseudogroup level. Management should stay in close tune with the group participants and give them as much to say about managing and ways and means as possible and avoid assuming the burden of caring for the group and assume the role and keep it as servants of the group, at the actual command of that group.

Management and enterprises are most highly successful when they attain most energetically toward true group status.

---

51. **Republic:** the Weimar Republic, the existing government of Germany prior to Hitler's rise to power in the early '30s.

52. **irascible:** easily provoked to anger; very irritable.

53. **mad dog:** fanatic or unreasonably zealous in beliefs, opinions or pursuits; literally, like a mad dog (a dog with rabies).

54. **chary:** cautious or careful; wary.

There are certain definite and precise laws by which management can raise the level of its own efficiency and the level of production and activity of a group.

When it is necessary to establish a surprise element in an attack or to secure a portion of the group from attack, suppression of *operational data* is permissible to management. Suppression of any other than operational data can disrupt a group and blow management over. Any management which operates as a censorship or a propaganda medium will inevitably destroy itself and injure the group. A management must not pervert affinity, communication or reality and must not interrupt it. A management fails in ratio to the amount of perversion or severance of ARC it engages upon, and its plans and the goals of the group are wrong in the exact ratio it finds itself "forced" to engage upon ARC perversion or severance of ARC in terms of propaganda or internal relations.

A management can instantly improve the tone of any organization and thus its efficiency by hooking up and keeping wide open all communication lines—communication lines between all departments and amongst all persons of the group and communication lines between the goal maker and the group. Fail to establish and keep in open and flowing condition one communication channel and the organization will fail to just that extent.

Communication lines are severed in this fashion: (a) by permitting so much entheta to flow on them that the group will close them or avoid them; (b) by perverting the communication and so invalidating the line that afterwards none will pay attention to the line; (c) by glutting the line with too much volume of traffic (too much material for too little meaning); and (d) by chopping the line through carelessness or malice or to gain authority (the principal reason, that last, why lines get tampered with).

He who holds the power of an organization is that person who holds its communication lines and who is a crossroad of the communications. Therefore, in a true group, communications and communication lines should be and are sacred. Communication lines are sacred. They have been considered so instinctively since the oldest ages of man. Messengers, heralds and riders have been the object of the greatest care even between combatants on enMEST missions. Priesthoods hold their power through posing or being communication relay points between gods and men. And even most governments consider cults sacred. Communication lines are sacred and who would interrupt or pervert a communication line within a group is entitled to group death—exile. And that usually happens as a natural course of events. Communication lines are sacred. They must not be used as channels of viciousness and entheta. They must not be twisted or perverted. They must not be glutted with many words and little meaning. They must not be severed. They must be established wherever a communication line seems to want to exist or is needed.

Any management of anything can raise tone and efficiency by establishing and maintaining zealously, as a sacred trust, communication lines through all the group and from outside the group into the group and from in the group outside the group.

The most vital lines of a group are not operational lines, although this may appear so to management. They are the theta lines between any theta and the group and the goal maker and the group. Management that tampers with these lines in any way will destroy itself. These actually have tension and explosion in them. It is as inevitable as nightfall that these lines will explode, when tampered with, at the exact point of the tampering. This is a natural law of communication lines.

A line is as dangerous to tamper with as it has truth in its channel. It is safe and even preserving of a line to cut it when it contains entheta. For example, when a true line is cut, it charges a little power into the cutter and he has authority for a moment thereby. But it is only the authority of the cut line. If the line is thus made to perish, the cutter loses his authority. If there is much truth in that line, it does not give authority to the cutter, it explodes him.

A group has the right to exile anyone it discovers to be guilty of tampering with any communication line.

A management which will pervert an affinity or sever one may gain a momentary power but the laws here are the same as those relating to communication, and an affinity tampered with will lower the tone of a group.

A management which will pervert or suppress a reality, no matter how "reasonable" the act seems, is acting in the direction of the destruction of a group. It is not what management thinks the group or the goal maker should know, it is what is true. A primary function of management is the discovery and publication, in the briefest form which will admit the whole force of the data, the reality of all existing circumstances, situations and personnel. A management which will hide data, even in the hope of sparing someone's feelings, is operating toward a decline of the group.

A true group must have a management which deals in affinity, reality and communication, and any group is totally within its rights, when a full and reasonable examination discloses management in fault of perverting or cutting ARC, of slaughtering, exiling or suspending that management. ARC is sacred.

Management should be cognizant of the differences existing in power. Management undeniably must have power but a management which confuses authority with power is acting, no matter its "sincerity" or "earnestness" or even conscious belief that it is doing what is right and well, in the direction of decay of organizational efficiency. Power which is held and used by rationale alone is almost imperishable. That power deteriorates and becomes ineffective in exact ratio to the amount of pain or punishment drive[55] it must use to accomplish its end. The theta of management becomes entheta in a dwindling spiral[56] once this course is entered upon. For example, the punishment of criminals creates more criminals. The use of punishment drive on the insane creates more insane. Punishment drive against inefficiency creates more inefficiency, and no management wisdom or power under the sun can reverse or interrupt this working law.

Every management of past ages has been an enturbulated group rule seeking to rule an enturbulated group. Management has only succeeded when punishment drive was suspended or when theta moved in over the scene from a goal maker and, by sheer theta power, disenturbulated the group. The need of management is for power to advance secondary and vital plans and coordinate their execution by the group.

The only power that ever works is derived from reason and the ability to reason. MEST surrenders only to reason when it is to become organized MEST. Punishment drive creates enMEST where MEST was sought. It is the boasted desire of every management to

---

55. **punishment drive:** pain, deprivation or other unpleasant consequence imposed on or experienced by an organism responding incorrectly under specific conditions so that, through avoidance, the desired learning or behavior becomes established.

56. **dwindling spiral:** a phenomenon of ARC whereby when one breaks some affinity, a little bit of the reality goes down, and then communication goes down, which makes it impossible to get affinity as high as before; so a little bit more gets knocked off affinity, and then reality goes down, and then communication. This is the dwindling spiral in progress, until it hits the bottom—death—which is no affinity, no communication and no reality. *See also* **ARC** in the glossary.

acquire MEST for the group. By employing punishment drive on the group or on MEST a management can acquire only entheta control of enMEST and that is death. Management, if enough free theta exists in the group or if the goal is sufficiently theta, can get away with punishment drive and can confuse the punishment drive it is applying with the existing theta in the group and can delude itself into thinking that accomplishment occurs because of punishment drive, not because of existing theta. Thus enthused about punishment drive, management then applies more of it with the result that the existing theta is enturbulated. Sooner or later the group perishes or, fortunate group, saves itself with a revolt which carries a theta goal. (Example: British navy, bad conditions of discipline before first quarter of nineteenth century; mutiny of whole navy for humanitarian handling of men; result, a more efficient navy than Britain had ever had before.)

Power, and very real, forceful power it is, can be sustained only when it deals with theta goals and is derived from theta principles. Authoritarian power, held by breaking or perverting ARC, enforced by punishment drive, brings to management certain destruction and brings to the group reduced efficiency or death.

One, in considering these things, is not dealing in airy philosophic impracticalities but in facts so hard and solid they can be worn and eaten and used as roofs. We are dealing here with the basic stuff of management and group survival. It is to be commented upon that management has succeeded despite its use of punishment drive and because of existing theta goals whether management knew it or not. This sums up not particularly to the discredit of managements of the past but to the highly resistant character of theta goals. Management, failing to understand the true force of its power and the source of that power, seeing only that if it cut and perverted ARC it had power of a sort, has been the yoke around the neck of mankind in most instances, not the proud thing management thinks it is or could be, keeping the wheels turning. Where wheels turned in the past it was usually because of highly vital theta goals, and thoroughly despite management. Management, being a needful cog in the scheme of things, has been kept around by a hopeful mankind on the off chance that it someday might be of complete use. A punishment-drive management is the spoke in the wheel of an action being conducted by a goal maker and a group, not the grease for the wheel which management sincerely believes itself to be. A goal maker–group combination action is only enturbulated because of the lack of a good management or the existence, much worse, of a punishment-drive management. Man would run better entirely unmanaged than in the hands of an authoritarian management, for the end of such a management is group death. A group theta-managed with real theta power would run better than a group entirely unmanaged.

Management derives power most swiftly by acting as interpreter between a goal maker and a group. The power of the management is effective in ratio to the cleanness with which it relays between the goal maker and the group on ARC. Management loses real power in the ratio that it perverts or cuts lines between the goal maker and the group. When the goal maker exists now only as a printed code, management can continue to prosper and can continue to serve only in the ratio that it keeps that code cleanly interpreted between archives and group. Management deteriorates and grows unprosperous in the ratio that it perverts or cuts the lines from code to group.

There is an intriguing factor involved, however: ARC lines. When they are slightly interrupted they deliver power to the individual that interrupts them. True, it is authoritarian power, death power. But a very faint tampering with a line gives authority to the tamperer since he is obscuring to some slight degree a section of theta. His group is trying to see the theta and reach it and if they can do so only through the tamperer and if they are convinced that the tamperer or tampering is necessary (which it *never* is, and the action of convincing them is part of tampering with such lines), then the group tolerates the tamperer in the hope of seeing more theta. Mistaking this regard for him as something he is receiving personally, the tamperer cannot resist, if he is a narrow and stupid man, tampering a little more with the ARC line. He can live and is tolerated only so long as the theta he is partially masking is not entirely obscured. But he, by that first tampering, starts on the dwindling spiral. Eventually he is so "reactive"[57] (and he would have to be pretty much reactive mind[58] to start such an operation) that he obscures the theta or discredits it. At that moment he dies. He has put so much tension on the line that it explodes. If it is not a very theta ARC in the first place, he is relatively safe for a long period. The pomp and glory he assumes are not his. He makes them enMEST and entheta and eventually corrupts them utterly and corrupts himself and all around him and dies as management.

There is also a pretense of having a theta goal without having one, which intrigues management. Lacking the actual article, the management postulates merely the fact that such an article exists and that management is the sole purveyor of this theta goal. Usually such a management makes excuses for the goal not being in sight or existing by claiming that "it is too complicated for ignorant minds to grasp," "it is too sacred to be defiled[59] by the hands of the mob." Management dresses itself in

---

57. **reactive:** irrational, reacting instead of acting.

58. **reactive mind:** that portion of a person's mind which works on a totally stimulus-response basis, which is not under his volitional control and which exerts force and the power of command over his awareness, purposes, thoughts, body and actions.

59. **defiled:** rendered morally foul or polluted; the ideal purity of (something) destroyed; corrupted; tainted.

all the trappings of a theta relay station, but as there is no theta goal in the first place to give to the group, punishment drive has to be entered upon instantly. Hellfire has to be promised to those who won't believe a theta goal exists just over management's shoulder. A flog has to be used to convince the group that the cause is just.

However, a group is capable of generating some theta on its own. There are always some minor goal makers around. Unfortunately these serve to buoy up a masking management by actually putting some theta into circulation. Management can then keep on masking an empty altar. But as the altar is empty, such a management is always afraid instinctively. It starts to speak of rabble, the mob, the horrors of individual say in group actions. It speaks of anarchy and uses wild propaganda to stampede and enturbulate its group. The life goes to some degree down in every individual in that group and stays up only because of the minor goal makers in the group. Management, seeing here a rival or a threat of discovery that it exists not for the goal but for itself, starts in punishment-driving the minor theta makers, calling them revolutionaries whenever they advance a goal or idea and having them torn down from any tiny eminence to which their meager supply of theta has lifted them. When the last of these goal makers is dead, the group is dead, management is dead and desolation reigns. *This has been the cycle of management amongst man since first he became civilized,* save in those times and places where a real goal maker existed and where management actually began by being a part of a nearly true group. (See the history of Greece, the history of Egypt, the history of Rome; trace the course of Greek tyrannies. See also the history of various companies, and one readily sorts out those which began because of a goal maker and those which pretended a goal existed but had no goal maker for the group but

only made goals for individuals—management itself. Three life insurance companies began because of real goal makers and they are the leading companies of America despite subsequent perversions of the goal and its subordination to individual profit.)

Now, it so happens that a culture which has within it many examples of punishment-drive masked management will begin to develop a spurious technology of management based upon mimicry of these masked punishment-drive managements. The technology is most ably put forward in Machiavelli's *Prince*[60] for that period. Almost any text on "military science" is a technology of masked management. However, such texts exist and are useful because they furnish a short-term method of assembling a unit to follow a cause whenever one appears. The technology of how a company evolutes[61] or a battery[62] spots[63] is not the technology of management but the technology of a coordinated group. Everywhere one looks in such a text on actual battle skill one finds cooperation and understanding is the essence and that ARC is stressed amongst the group itself at every period and paragraph. But alas, the technology of the military management itself is so far from useful or factual that wars get won only because most armies have the same management system and that one wins

---

60. **Machiavelli's** *Prince:* refers to *Il Principe* (*The Prince*), a famous work on the principles of authoritarian rule by Niccolo Machiavelli (1469–1527), an Italian author and political philosopher.

61. **evolutes:** makes a tactical movement, such as the unfolding or opening out of a body of troops or squadron of ships; makes a movement or change of position, such as counter-marching (a movement in which a file or column reverses its direction, the individuals remaining in the same order and position), etc., required in the due disposition of a force, whether for review or for active operations.

62. **battery:** a tactical unit of artillery, usually consisting of six guns together with the artillerymen, equipment, etc. required to operate them.

63. **spots:** determines (a location) precisely on either the ground or a map.

which makes less errors than another and which has a better "cause."

For example, the communist main group in Russia is not a true group. Probably the United States is much closer to (but very far from) a true group. Thus the nation of Russia versus the nation of the United States, in a battle of culture, would lose miserably. But an army of communists working for a management which only recently lost its goal makers, Marx and Lenin,[64] can have a "cause" couched[65] in modern terms. All armies are considerably entheta and take only enMEST. But a Russian army has a "cause" superior to a US army. Neither army has a true group cause, but the United States "cause" has not been restated in convincing modern terms. A second-rate and obsolete cause is as dangerous to have around an army as an obsolete weapon. The US army "cause" does not include a conquest-of-MEST clause but contains only protection-of-status-quo clauses. Once the United States drove hard on theta goals. Because her people and culture are not much decayed and her technology is high, a United States with a *cause*, as before, could easily outreach any Russian culture. And a United States army with such a cause would crush a vastly superior Russian force.

Armies, understand, are short-term groups intimately concerned with the conquest of MEST, which, no matter if they made enMEST of it, is still a MEST goal until conquered. Thus armies can be thrown into action with far less reason than a culture, and, not so closely, ARC within the unit itself can be catalyzed. An

---

64. **Lenin:** Vladimir I. Lenin (1870–1924), Russian communist leader. He was an agitator for socialism. During World War I he urged socialists in all countries to rise against their own governments, and he assumed leadership of the Russian Revolution in 1917.

65. **couched:** arranged or framed (words, a sentence, etc.); put into words; expressed.

army, then, builds its technology on fantastically high ARC on the private-corporal level and is governed by a fantastically low ARC on the management level, because ARC is high in the bulk of the group and is commanded to be high (management of armies would reverse such a thing if they knew what they were effecting, one fears) by a low-ARC management. Optimum in armies is that high ARC on the private-corporal level and management by a government which has high-theta goals and is itself high ARC. When this is attained armies explode out of Asia Minor and overrun Europe.

With such bad examples in a culture, management can develop an entirely false technology. Managers have to be geniuses to work with such technologies and ordinarily work themselves into a swift demise, as witness the presidents of the United States, who can be seen, if you compare the pictures of the same president after just two years of being president, to deteriorate swiftly. The group one way or another will try to knock apart an authoritarian management or a management even slightly authoritarian. The management thinks this is all because of bad planning, tries to plan better, and thinks all can be righted by just a little more emergency punishment drive. The group revolts more. Management punishment-drives more. And finally something has to explode. It is a lucky nation which blows into a theta-goal revolt early in this cycle. The government of the United States is overworked and inefficient as management because all the principles of its original goal makers are not applied and those that are applied are slightly perverted. And the same thing obtains with Russian management. (Example: Read the works of Paine and the works of Jefferson in their original form and read also the letters and personal opinions of these men. You will find more theta in those writings which has been overlooked than the whole US government is using from those same goal makers. Read Marx and Lenin and look at the tremendous quantity of theta untapped in those works.)

Bad management, then, like any aberration,[66] goes by contagion. Because of a native existence of theta goals even as to common survival, and a country wealthy in brilliant people and natural resources, management can become a sort of priesthood because success reigns and management has never been loath[67] to take credit for a group's production. But statistics will tell you swiftly that the great god "modern business management" is in continual trouble, is expensive, is uneconomical, and that, by the duration of large fortunes and businesses on the average, such management as has been purporting to be management is almost a complete failure and is murdering outright the majority of enterprises of this country. The rise of unionism[68] is not an index of the viciousness and willfulness of man but is, as it rises and wars against production, an index of the failure of management as it has been practiced as a technology. Unionism is not wrong. It is simply an unnecessary arbitrary existing because of the existing arbitrary of management operating on an authoritarian level, masking the absence of theta goal makers and seeking to enforce that lack with punishment drive.

America fought for independence from absentee management in 1776 and won. With the advent of Alexander Hamilton's

---

66. **aberration:** a departure from rational thought or behavior. It means basically to err, to make mistakes, or more specifically to have fixed ideas which are not true. The word is also used in its scientific sense. It means departure from a straight line. If a line should go from A to B, then if it is *aberrated* it would go from A to some other point, to some other point, to some other point, to some other point, to some other point, and finally arrive at B. Taken in its scientific sense, it would also mean the lack of straightness or to see crookedly as, for example, a man sees a horse but thinks he sees an elephant. Aberrated conduct would be wrong conduct, or conduct not supported by reason. Aberration is opposed to sanity, which would be its opposite. From the Latin, *aberrare,* to wander from; Latin, *ab,* away, *errare,* to wander.

67. **loath:** unwilling; reluctant; disinclined; averse.

68. **unionism:** the system, principles or methods of groups designed to protect and advance the interests of wage and salary workers, particularly in large industrial and commercial concerns of the Western world.

119

banking system[69] (a medal please for Burr,[70] traitor though he may have been) that part of independence related to economics did a marked and remarkable slump back into the dark ages of fascism—or tyranny, as they called it in those days. Senator Bone, USS,[71] once remarked to me, "I have fought since 1905 to place public utilities in the hands of the people. But I believe that, by giving them at last to the government, I have exchanged a fairly unreasonable for a very unreasonable master. It seems to me that when this country got rid of slavery in the Civil War we changed an outright form of slavery for a far more insidious brand—the tyranny of modern management." Fascism exists in America as almost the sole modus operandi of big business. And fascism or authoritarianism almost always murders itself swiftly since it is entheta and enturbulates the existing theta. This is best exemplified by the management-labor upsets which have been increasing in volume since the early 1900s.

Economic tyranny alone could make possible the far less than ideal group ideology[72] of communism. Where fascistic[73]

---

69. **Alexander Hamilton's banking system:** Alexander Hamilton (1755–1804), as first Secretary of the US Treasury (1789–1797), initiated a strong central banking system controlled by the federal government and federal taxes on imports and exports.

70. **Burr:** Aaron Burr (1756–1836), American soldier and statesman. A political enemy of Alexander Hamilton, Burr challenged Hamilton to a duel and mortally wounded him in 1804. Burr was tried for treason in 1807, and though he was acquitted, never regained the confidence of the people.

71. **USS:** United States Senate.

72. **ideology:** a systematic scheme of ideas, usually relating to politics or society or to the conduct of a class or group, and regarded as justifying actions, especially one that is held implicitly or adopted as a whole and maintained regardless of the course of events.

73. **fascistic:** of or having to do with a governmental system led by a dictator having complete power, forcibly suppressing opposition and criticism, regimenting all industry, commerce, etc., and emphasizing an aggressive nationalism and often racism.

business management exists, there socialism[74] and communism can go. State ownership of everything including the human soul, and a communal ideology conducted with false propaganda by a rather fascistic group in Moscow, are equally undesirable. The world is in tumult today because of three schools of management: fascism reserves the right to fire at will, and devil take the men of production; socialism outlaws private property and builds up staggering bureaucracies about as efficient as Rube Goldberg's machinery;[75] communism buffoons around with one-time high ethic tenets, building an empire on deceits. None of the three are worthy of attention should a workable science of management come into being.

Such a science of management should obtain optimum performance potentialities and optimum living conditions for the group and its members. Such a science is postulated here. It is not an ideology. It is an effort toward rational operation of groups.

In accordance with an ambition to put its house in order, it is suggested that any organization so desiring put into practice the following tenets:

1. Consider well its ideal and ethics. This is the province of goal making.

2. Consider well its rationale. This is the province of management, its planning and coordination.

---

74. **socialism:** a theory or policy of social organization which aims at or advocates the ownership and control of the means of production, capital, land, property, etc., by the community as a whole, and their administration or distribution in the interests of all.

75. **Rube Goldberg's machinery:** cartoon mechanical devices of absurdly unnecessary complexity drawn by Rube Goldberg (1883–1970), American cartoonist.

---

3.   Consider well its execution. This is the province of staff and individual members of the group.

4.   Establish a general, flexible plan of government—adopting a constitution, selecting its officers with full agreement, adhering to its establishment and establishers.

5.   Ever lean toward creative and constructive goals and execute its ventures creatively and constructively as opposed to "saving things," "arbitrary emergencies," and destructive planning and action.

6.   Choose for its posts of trust high-theta personnel who plan creatively and constructively in expanding terms rather than "emergency" terms. Keep out of office the death-talkers who pervert or selectively censor communications or cut lines to gain power, who postulate opportunistic but dire realities and who, perverting affinity, have no love for man.

7.   Hook up an abundance of communication lines to fill their various needs, keep the communications terse, keep the communications wholly honest and drop no curtains between the organization and the public about anything.

8.   Incline in the direction of creating affinity from group to group and group to management. Create and maintain high affinity with the rest of the world.

9.   Create a high and ethical reality of a better world and then make it come into being. Make the organization a model of that better world.

10. Persevere in the continual raising of group tone. Persevere toward the goal of the highest individual tone. It is theoretically true that a high enough group tone level almost nullifies the necessity of individual clearing[76] and that high individual tone creates a high group tone.

11. Self-generate the organization into a model of efficiency in all its departments and with high pride in his performance on the part of every individual member of the group.

12. Operate on the principle that the failure, in any department, of one individual or subgroup, by contagion, threatens the survival of all.

13. Understand thoroughly the principle that the amount of theta in the group materially determines the longevity, greatness and general survival of that group and its members and that the amount of entheta in the group determines its proximity to death, and thus have done with the casualnesses and insincerities existing in a low-toned outer society.

---

76. **clearing:** a gradient process of finding places where attention is fixed and restoring the ability of a person to place and remove attention under his own determinism (according to his own choice).

10

The Credo of a Good and Skilled Manager

10

The Credo of a Good and Skilled Manager

To be effective and successful a manager must:

1. Understand as fully as possible the goals and aims of the group he manages. He must be able to see and embrace the *ideal* attainment of the goal as envisioned by a goal maker. He must be able to tolerate and better the *practical* attainments and advances of which his group and its members may be capable. He must strive to narrow, always, the ever-existing gulf between the *ideal* and the *practical*.

2. He must realize that a primary mission is the full and honest interpretation by himself of the ideal and ethic and their goals and aims to his subordinates and the group itself. He must lead creatively and persuasively toward these goals his subordinates, the group itself and the individuals of the group.

3. He must embrace the organization and act solely for the entire organization and never form or favor cliques. His judgment of individuals of the group should be solely in the light of their worth to the entire group.

4. He must never falter in sacrificing individuals to the good of the group both in planning and execution and in his justice.

5. He must protect all established communication lines and complement them where necessary.

6. He must protect all affinity in his charge and have himself an affinity for the group itself.

7. He must attain always to the highest creative reality.

8. His planning must accomplish, in the light of goals and aims, the activity of the entire group. He must never let organizations grow and sprawl[1] but, learning by pilots,[2] must keep organizational planning fresh and flexible.

9. He must recognize in himself the rationale of the group and receive and evaluate the data out of which he makes his solutions with the highest attention to the truth of that data.

10. He must constitute[3] himself on the orders of service to the group.

11. He must permit himself to be served well as to his individual requirements, practicing an economy of his own efforts and enjoying certain comforts to the wealth of keeping high his rationale.

---

1. **sprawl:** spread out in a straggling or disordered fashion.

2. **pilots:** preliminary or experimental trials or tests.

3. **constitute:** establish or set up; make (a person or thing) something.

12. He should require of his subordinates that they relay into their own spheres of management the whole and entire of his true feelings and the reasons for his decisions as clearly as they can be relayed and expanded and interpreted only for the greater understanding of the individuals governed by those subordinates.

13. He must never permit himself to pervert or mask any portion of the ideal and ethic on which the group operates nor must he permit the ideal and ethic to grow old and outmoded and unworkable. He must never permit his planning to be perverted or censored by subordinates. He must never permit the ideal and ethic of the group's individual members to deteriorate, using always reason to interrupt such a deterioration.

14. He must have faith in the goals, faith in himself and faith in the group.

15. He must lead by demonstrating always creative and constructive subgoals. He must not drive by threat and fear.

16. He must realize that every individual in the group is engaged in some degree in the managing of other men, life and MEST and that a liberty of management within this code should be allowed to every such submanager.

Thus conducting himself, a manager can win empire for his group, whatever that empire may be.

Appendix

Tone Scale

4.0   Eagerness, Exhilaration

3.5   Strong Interest

3.0   Conservatism

2.5   Boredom

2.0   Antagonism (Overt Hostility)

1.5   Anger

1.1   Covert Hostility

1.0   Fear

0.5   Grief

0.2   Apathy

0.0   Death

About the Author

L. Ron Hubbard is one of the most acclaimed and widely read authors of all time, primarily because his works express a firsthand knowledge of the realities of life and what it really takes to accomplish something in it—knowledge gained not from standing on the sidelines but through lifelong experience with people from all walks of life.

As Ron said, "One doesn't learn about life by sitting in an ivory tower, thinking about it. One learns about life by being part of it." And that is how he lived.

He began his pursuit of knowledge at a very early age. When he was eight years old he was already well on his way to being a seasoned traveler. His adventures included voyages to China, Japan and other points in the Orient and South Pacific, covering a quarter of a million miles by the age of nineteen. In the course of his travels he became closely acquainted with twenty-one different races and cultures all over the world.

In the fall of 1930, Ron pursued his studies of mathematics and engineering, enrolling at George Washington University where he was also a member of one of the first American classes on nuclear physics. He realized that neither the East nor the West contained the full answer to the problems of existence. Despite all of mankind's advances in the physical sciences, a *workable* technology of the mind and life had never been developed. Ron took on the responsibility of filling that gap in man's knowledge.

He financed his early research through fiction writing. He became one of the most highly demanded authors in the golden age of popular adventure and science fiction writing during the 1930s and 1940s, interrupted only by his service in the US Navy during World War II.

Partially disabled at the war's end, Ron applied what he had learned from his researches. He made breakthroughs and developed techniques which made it possible for him to recover from his injuries and help others to regain their health. It was during this time that the basic tenets of Dianetics technology were codified.

In 1948, he wrote a manuscript detailing his discoveries. It was not published at that time, but circulated amongst Ron's friends, who copied it and passed it on to others. (This manuscript was formally published in 1951 as *Dianetics: The Original Thesis* and later republished as *The Dynamics of Life*.) The interest generated by this manuscript prompted a flood of requests for more information on the subject, and the steadily increasing flow of letters asking that he detail more applications of his new technology resulted in Ron spending all his time answering letters. He decided to write and publish a comprehensive text on the subject—*Dianetics: The Modern Science of Mental Health.* When the book was released—9 May 1950—it immediately shot to the top of the *New York Times* bestseller list, remaining there month after month.

Ron's work did not stop with the success of *Dianetics* but accelerated, with new discoveries and breakthroughs a constant, normal occurrence. In his further research he discovered the very nature of life itself and its exact relationship to this universe. These discoveries led to his development of Scientology, the first workable technology for the improvement of conditions in any aspect of life.

Throughout his life, Ron was a leader of men. As a captain of ships and as the head of expeditions to Alaska, the Caribbean and the Mediterranean, he recognized the need for administrative and organizational technology in order to improve efficiency and effectiveness within a group. Therefore, when Scientology's expansion threatened to outdistance its organization, Ron intervened, applying his understanding of the basics of life to the fields of management and administration. He discovered fundamental laws which, if violated, caused the collapse of groups. From his research he developed and codified a complete management and administrative technology which allows any organization to expand limitlessly.

Applying this technology, organizations around the world are capable of expansion and growth on a rapid but stable basis. Executives using the basics and principles which Ron discovered can easily deal with the situations and problems which stand in the way of expansion.

Ron's work continued through the early 1980s, amassing an enormous volume of material on the mind and life totalling over 60 million words—recorded in books, manuscripts and taped lectures. Today this technology is studied and applied daily in hundreds of Scientology churches, missions and organizations around the world. With his research fully completed and codified, L. Ron Hubbard departed his body on 24 January 1986.

Ron not only opened a new door to personal ability for mankind; he also made it possible for organizations of any kind to forge their own way to success and predictably achieve their goals.

Glossary

Aberration: a departure from rational thought or behavior. It means basically to err, to make mistakes, or more specifically to have fixed ideas which are not true. The word is also used in its scientific sense. It means departure from a straight line. If a line should go from A to B, then if it is *aberrated* it would go from A to some other point, to some other point, to some other point, to some other point, to some other point, and finally arrive at B. Taken in its scientific sense, it would also mean the lack of straightness or to see crookedly as, for example, a man sees a horse but thinks he sees an elephant. Aberrated conduct would be wrong conduct, or conduct not supported by reason. Aberration is opposed to sanity, which would be its opposite. From the Latin, *aberrare*, to wander from; Latin, *ab*, away, *errare*, to wander.

adjutant: an officer in the army whose business it is to assist the superior officers by receiving and communicating orders, conducting correspondence and the like.

affinity: degree of liking or affection or lack of it. Affinity is a tolerance of distance. A great affinity would be a tolerance of or liking of close proximity. A lack of affinity would be an intolerance of or dislike of close proximity. Affinity is one of the components of understanding. *See also* **ARC** in this glossary.

Alexander: Alexander the Great (356–23 B.C.), king of Macedonia, an ancient kingdom located in what is now Greece and Yugoslavia.

Alexander Hamilton's banking system: Alexander Hamilton (1755–1804), as first Secretary of the US Treasury (1789–97), initiated a strong central banking system controlled by the federal government and federal taxes on imports and exports.

amphibious: designating, of or for a military operation involving the landing of assault troops on a shore from seaborne transports.

apprised: given notice; informed; advised.

arborvitae: any of several ornamental or timber-producing evergreen trees of the cypress family, native to North America and eastern Asia, having a scaly bark and scalelike leaves on branchlets.

ARC: a word made from the initial letters of *Affinity, Reality* and *Communication* which together equate to understanding. These are the three things necessary to the understanding of something—one has to have some affinity for it, it has to be real to him to some degree and he needs some communication with it before he can understand it. *See also* **affinity, reality** and **communication** in this glossary. For more information on ARC, read the book *The Problems of Work* by L. Ron Hubbard.

ARC breaks: sudden drops or cuttings of a person's affinity, reality or communication with someone or something. Up-sets with people or things (ARC breaks) come about because of a lessening or sundering (breaking apart) of affinity, reality, or communication or understanding. It is called an ARC break instead of an upset, because if one discovers which of the three points of understanding have been cut, one can bring about a rapid recovery in the person's state of mind. *See also* **ARC** in this glossary.

ardures: a coined word meaning strong efforts; hard work to accomplish or achieve. Formed from the word *arduous*, derived from Latin *ardu-us*, which means "high, steep, difficult."

armament: war equipment and supplies.

arsenals: government establishments where military equipment or munitions are manufactured.

asperity: harshness or sharpness of tone, temper or manner; severity.

assimilated: taken in and absorbed or incorporated into the system.

attendant: accompanying as a circumstance or result.

authoritarians: persons who advocate, practice or enforce un-questioning obedience to authority, as that of a dictator, rather than individual freedom of judgment and action.

balk: stop, as at an obstacle, and refuse to proceed or to do something specified.

bane: cause of death, ruin or harm; curse.

barrooms: establishments or rooms with a bar for the serving of alcoholic beverages.

bask: lie in or expose oneself to a pleasant warmth or atmosphere; used figuratively meaning to take pleasure or enjoyment (in).

battery: (1) a group of similar things arranged, connected or used together; set or series; array. Also refers to the personnel who operate such equipment. (2) a tactical unit of artillery, usually consisting of six guns together with the artillerymen, equipment, etc., required to operate them.

befuddlement: confusion; muddle.

blue pencil: a pencil (traditionally blue), used to make corrections, deletions, etc., as in editing a manuscript.

boiling, keep (something): keep anything going (from the agitated motion of boiling water); in this sense, ensuring that an order is not just dropped or forgotten, but is kept moving toward completion.

bottleneck: any point at which movement or progress is slowed up because much must be funneled through it.

brass-banded: loudly and resoundingly promoted, as with bands (such as military bands) made up of brass and percussion instruments.

Burr: Aaron Burr (1756–1836), American soldier and statesman. A political enemy of Alexander Hamilton, Burr challenged Hamilton to a duel and mortally wounded him in 1804. Burr was tried for treason in 1807, and though he was acquitted, never regained the confidence of the people.

calling: one's occupation, profession or trade.

caravan: of a group of travelers, as merchants or pilgrims, journeying together for safety in passing through deserts, hostile territory, etc.

carpet, on the: in the position of being reprimanded by one in authority.

catalyzes: changes, brings about or hastens a result, due to the stimulus of another thing or person.

cause: the point of emanation (something coming forth from a source). It could be defined also for purposes of communication, as source-point. If you consider a river flowing to the sea, the place where it began would be the source-point or *cause*, and the place where it went into the sea would be the effect-point and the sea would be the effect of the river. The man firing the gun is *cause*; the man receiving the bullet is effect.

chary: cautious or careful; wary.

chimeras: often fantastic combinations of incongruous parts, especially those calculated to deceive. The term comes from the name of a monster, the *Chimera*, in Greek mythology which breathed fire and had a serpent's tail, a goat's body and a lion's head.

clarion call: a loud and clear call or summons; a ringing speech, phrase, etc., that stirs to action. A *clarion* is a shrill-sounding trumpet with a narrow tube, formerly much used as a signal in war.

clearing: a gradient process of finding places where attention is fixed and restoring the ability of a person to place and remove attention under his own determinism (according to his own choice).

coalesces: unites or comes together, so as to form one.

collectivism: the socialistic theory of the collective ownership or control of all the means of production, and especially of the land, by the whole community or state, i.e., the people collectively, for the benefit of the people as a whole. *See also* **socialism** in this glossary.

combat information centers: agencies found on most major combat vessels which coordinate the activities of naval departments and divisions during preparations for battle and in actual battle (abbreviated *CIC*). CIC is the sensory center of the ship, the place in which tactical information is gathered and evaluated, and action coordinated. Specifically, CIC is charged with the responsibility of gathering all possible information concerning friendly or enemy ships or aircraft within range of the equipment, evaluating this information, delivering parts of the evaluated information to appropriate stations aboard ship and controlling tactical units.

comm: short for **communication** (see next entry in glossary).

communication: the interchange of ideas across space. Its full definition is the consideration and action of impelling an impulse or particle from source-point across a distance to receipt-point, with the intention of bringing into being at the receipt-point a duplication and understanding of that which emanated from the source-point. The formula of communication is cause, distance, effect, with intention, attention and duplication with understanding.

communication lines: (abbreviated **comm lines**) the routes along which a communication travels from one person to another; the lines on which particles flow; any sequences through which a message of any character may go. *See also* **communication** in this glossary.

communications: means of sending messages, orders, etc., including telegraph, telephone, radio and television. The definition of *communication* is the interchange of ideas across space. Its full definition is the consideration and action of impelling an impulse or particle from source-point across a distance to receipt-point, with the intention of bringing into being at the receipt-point a duplication and understanding of that which emanated from the source-point. The formula of communication is cause, distance, effect, with intention, attention and duplication with understanding.

communicator: one who keeps communication lines moving or controlled for an executive. The communicator is to help the executive free his or her time for essential income earning actions, rest or recreation, and to prolong the term of appointment of the executive by safeguarding against overload. The communicator's job includes more than secretarial duties, as the communicator is responsible for policing unusual and unnecessary traffic on the executive's lines and for ensuring that the executive's orders are complied with.

compass course: a course whose bearing is relative to the meridian (one of the great circles of the Earth passing through the poles and any given point on the Earth's surface) as given by the navigator's compass, no compensation being made for variation or deviation.

congenitally: as the result of a condition present at birth, whether inherited or caused by the environment, especially the uterine environment.

consideration: thinking, believing, supposing. Consideration is the highest capability of life, taking rank over the mechanics of space, energy and time.

consignment: a shipment of goods sent to an agent for sale or safekeeping.

constitute: establish or set up; make (a person or thing) something.

convoy: accompany (a ship, fleet, supplies, etc.) in order to protect; escort.

couched: arranged or framed (words, a sentence, etc.); put into words; expressed.

county seats: towns or cities that are the centers of government of counties.

covert: characterized by concealed, hidden or disguised hostility; referring to a person at the level of *covert hostility* on the Tone Scale. (See Appendix, page 133.) Such an individual can be accurately spotted by his conversation, since he seeks only to enturbulate those around him, to upset them by his conversation, to destroy them without their ever being aware of his purpose. He listens only to data which will serve him in his enturbulations. Here is the gossip, here is the unfaithful wife, here is the card cheat; here is the most undesirable stratum of any social order. *See also* **Tone Scale** and **enturbulated** in this glossary.

Cross, city of the: the city of Jerusalem, where per the Bible, Jesus Christ was crucified on the cross.

cryptic: mysterious in meaning; puzzling; ambiguous.

defiled: rendered morally foul or polluted; the ideal purity of (something) destroyed; corrupted; tainted.

deigns: thinks it worthy of oneself (to do something); thinks fit; condescends.

deity: god or goddess.

despatch: a written message, particularly an official communication.

dispensary: a place where something is dealt out or distributed, especially medicines.

dissension: strong disagreement; contention or quarrel; discord.

dolts: dull, stupid people; blockheads.

duplication: the action of something being made, done or caused to happen again. Used in this sense to denote unnecessary or wasted motion. In Scientology, *duplication* is also used to describe the action of reproducing something exactly. For example, if Person A communicated the concept of a cat to Person B and Person B got the exact same concept of a cat without any alteration, Person B would be said to have *duplicated* what was originated by Person A.

dwindling spiral: a phenomenon of ARC whereby when one breaks some affinity, a little bit of the reality goes down, and then communication goes down, which makes it impossible to get affinity as high as before; so a little bit more gets knocked off affinity, and then reality goes down, and then communication. This is the dwindling spiral in progress, until it hits the bottom—death—which is no affinity, no communication and no reality. *See also* **ARC** in this glossary.

dynamics: there could be said to be eight urges (drives, impulses) in life, which we call *dynamics*. They are motives or motivations. We call them the eight dynamics. These are urges for survival as or through (1) self, (2) sex and family, (3) groups, (4) all mankind, (5) living things (plants and animals), (6) the material universe, (7) spirits, and (8) infinity or the Supreme Being. For more information on the dynamics, see the book *Scientology: The Fundamentals of Thought* by L. Ron Hubbard.

embark: set out on a venture; commence.

encroachments: intrusions (especially by insidious or gradual advances) on the territory, rights or accustomed sphere of action of others; gradual inroads made or extensions of boundaries at the expense of something else.

engrossed: occupied completely, as the mind or attention, absorbed.

enMEST: MEST which has been confused and enturbulated, and thereby rendered less usable. *See also* **enturbulated** and MEST in this glossary.

entheta: a coined word in Scientology, made from the words *en*turbulated *theta* (thought or life). As used here, it refers to communications which, based on lies and confusions, are slanderous, choppy or destructive in an attempt to overwhelm or suppress a person or group. *See also* **enturbulated** and **theta** in this glossary.

enturbulated: made turbulent or agitated and disturbed.

epistle: a communication made to an absent person in writing; a letter. Chiefly (from its use in translations from Latin and Greek) applied to letters written in ancient times, especially to those which rank as literary productions, or to those of a public character or addressed to a body of persons. Used with a playful or sarcastic implication in application to ordinary (modern) letters.

epitomizing: being representative or typical of the characteristics or general quality of a whole class.

ESP: extrasensory perception: perception or communication outside of normal sensory capability, as in telepathy and clairvoyance (the supernatural power of seeing objects or actions removed in space or time from natural viewing).

evolutes: makes a tactical movement, such as the unfolding or opening out of a body of troops or squadron of ships; makes a movement or change of position, such as countermarching (a movement in which a file or column reverses its direction, the individuals remaining in the same order and position), etc., required in the due disposition of a force, whether for review or for active operations.

executive: one who holds a position of administrative or managerial responsibility in an organization. To give one some idea of the power associated with the word, Noah Webster, in 1828, defined it as "The officer, whether king, president or other chief magistrate, who superintends the execution of the laws; the person who administers the government, executive power or authority in government." Executive is used in distinction from legislative and judicial. The body that deliberates and enacts laws is legislative; the body that judges or applies the laws to particular cases is judicial; the body or person who carries the laws into effect or superintends the enforcement of them is executive, according to its nineteenth-century governmental meaning according to Webster. The word comes from the Latin "*Ex(s)equi* (past participle *ex*[*s*]*ecutus*), execute, follow to the end: *ex-*, completely + *sequi*, to follow." In other words, he follows things to the end and *gets something done*.

falderol: mere nonsense; foolish talk or ideas.

fascistic: of or having to do with a governmental system led by a dictator having complete power, forcibly suppressing opposition and criticism, regimenting all industry, commerce, etc., and emphasizing an aggressive nationalism and often racism.

figurehead: a person who is head of a group, company, etc., in title and is a symbol of the goals of that group.

flow: a progress of energy between two points; an impulse or direction of energy particles or thought or masses between terminals; the progress of particles or impulse waves from Point A to Point B.

fodder: coarse food for cattle, horses, sheep, etc., as cornstalks, hay and straw.

Fulton: Robert Fulton (1765–1815), American engineer and inventor; builder of the first profitable steamboat.

Genghis Khan: (1162–1227) Mongol conqueror of most of Asia and of east Europe. He was known to be ruthless in war, but he built an empire which lasted until 1368.

girdling: encompassing, enclosing, encircling.

glut: fill (a receptacle, channel, pipe, etc.) to excess; choke up; saturate thoroughly with some substance.

goal-making: creating or establishing the aims, achievements or ends toward which effort is directed.

guidon: the identification flag of a military unit. Used figuratively.

harlots: prostitutes.

head of steam: literally, the pressure exerted by confined fluid, used to generate mechanical power. Used figuratively in this sense to mean being very excited or angry about something.

helmsman: the person who steers a ship.

hems and haws: makes sounds as if one is clearing the throat, or gropes around in speech, while searching for the right words.

herald: (formerly) a royal or official messenger, especially one representing a monarch in an ambassadorial capacity during wartime.

Hershey, Milton: (1857–1945) American industrialist, founder of a large chocolate-manufacturing business.

ideology: a systematic scheme of ideas, usually relating to politics or society or to the conduct of a class or group, and regarded as justifying actions, especially one that is held implicitly or adopted as a whole and maintained regardless of the course of events.

idiosyncrasies: characteristics, habits, mannerisms or the like that are peculiar to an individual.

implicit: necessarily or naturally involved though not plainly apparent or expressed; essentially a part or condition; inherent.

indoctrinating: instructing; teaching.

ineptness: lack of skill or aptitude for a particular task or assignment; awkwardness; clumsiness.

in lieu of: in place of; instead of.

insubordination: resistance to or defiance of authority; refusal to obey orders; disobedience.

integral: necessary for completeness; essential.

in toto: as a whole; in its entirety; totally; altogether.

inverse: (of a proportion) containing quantities of which an increase in one results in a decrease in another. A quantity is said to be in inverse proportion to another quantity if it increases as the other decreases, or vice versa.

inviolability: the quality or fact of being inviolable (not to be treated without proper respect or regard; not liable or allowed to suffer violence).

irascible: easily provoked to anger; very irritable.

jailbird: a person who is or has been confined in jail; convict or ex-convict.

Jefferson: Thomas Jefferson (1743–1826), third president of the United States. Jefferson wrote and presented the first draft of the Declaration of Independence in 1776.

junked: cast aside as junk; discarded as no longer of use; scrapped.

"Kit-Kat": a made-up name for a nightclub, an establishment for evening entertainment, generally open until the early morning, that serves liquor and usually food and offers patrons music, comedy acts, a floor show or dancing; nightspot.

lathe: a machine for shaping an article of wood, metal, etc., by holding and turning it rapidly against the edge of a cutting or abrading tool.

Lenin: Vladimir I. Lenin (1870–1924), Russian communist leader. He was an agitator for socialism. During World War I he urged socialists in all countries to rise against their own governments, and he assumed leadership of the Russian Revolution in 1917.

Lewis, John L.: (1880–1969) powerful labor leader in the United States from 1917 to 1940. Formerly president of the United Mine Workers, a labor movement to improve conditions for mine workers. Throughout World War II Lewis repeatedly called his miners out on strike, defying the government in many instances. In December 1946 a Federal court injunction was issued against the United Mine Workers, enjoining them to stop striking and levying fines of $3,500,000 against the group and $10,000 against Lewis personally.

line: the route along which particles travel between one terminal and the next in an organization; a fixed pattern of terminals who originate and receive or receive and relay orders, information or other particles. A line can be vertical such as a command line where authority and power of position increases the higher up one goes, or a line can be horizontal where each terminal on the line shares a similar status. *See also* **terminal** in this glossary.

loath: unwilling; reluctant; disinclined; averse.

Macedonian: of or having to do with Macedonia, an ancient country in the Balkan Peninsula, north of ancient Greece.

Machiavelli's *Prince*: refers to *Il Principe* (*The Prince*), a famous work on the principles of authoritarian rule by Niccolo Machiavelli (1469–1527), an Italian author and political philosopher.

mad dog: fanatic or unreasonably zealous in beliefs, opinions or pursuits; literally, like a mad dog (a dog with rabies).

manic: excessively excited or enthusiastic; crazed.

martyred: made into a martyr (a person who is put to death or endures great suffering on behalf of any belief, principle or cause).

Marx: Karl Marx (1818–83), German political philosopher, re-garded by some as founder of modern socialism. The work he is most known for is *The Communist Manifesto,* in which he states that the evils of capitalist society cannot be abol-ished by reform but only by the destruction of the whole capitalist economy and establishment of a new classless society.

message center: an office or other area where incoming and outgoing messages, mail, etc., are received and transmitted as by telephone, computer or messenger.

messiah: an expected liberator or savior of an oppressed people or country.

MEST: the physical universe. A word coined from the initial letters of *M*atter, *E*nergy, *S*pace and *T*ime, which are the component parts (elements) of the physical universe. Also used as an adjective, in the same sense to mean physical— as in "MEST universe," meaning the "physical universe."

mimeograph machines: duplicating machines for producing cop-ies from a stencil.

Mohammed: (A.D. 570–632) Arab prophet, founder of Islam, the prominent religion of Asia.

monopolize: obtain exclusive possession of, keep entirely to oneself.

mystic: of hidden meaning or nature; mysterious.

Napoleon: Napoleon Bonaparte (1769–1821), French military leader and emperor of France (1804–15).

nebulous: lacking form; hazy; vague; confused.

Nelson: Horatio Nelson (1758–1805), admiral in the English navy, known as one of the greatest of naval strategists.

neurone: individual cell of the nervous system which, though effectively in contact with other nerve cells, is a structurally distinct unit; used figuratively to describe the functioning and communication of an individual within a larger group.

neurotic: exhibiting behavior characteristic of one who is insane or disturbed on some subject (as opposed to a psychotic, who is just insane in general).

niagara: anything taken as resembling Niagara Falls (the falls of the Niagara River in Canada) in force and relentlessness; avalanche.

Nxw xs thx. . . . : an example illustrating an inoperational teletype, using the common typist's practice exercise, "Now is the time for all good men to come to the aid of the party."

obtain: be prevalent, customary, or in vogue; prevail.

offing, in the: in the projected future; likely to happen.

operative: a secret agent; spy.

organization: a number of persons or groups having specific responsibilities and united for some purpose or work; a number of terminals and communication lines united with a common purpose. The purpose keeps in contact with one another the terminals and the lines. An organization isn't a factory or a house. It isn't a machine or a product. It is something which has its own spirit. It is composed of people who are governed by certain rules and purposes and who know how to do their jobs.

Ouija board: (*trademark*) a device consisting of a small board on legs that rests on a larger board marked with words, letters of the alphabet, etc., and that by moving over the larger board and touching the words, letters, etc., while the fingers of spiritualists, mediums, or others rest lightly upon it, is employed to answer questions, give messages, etc.

outfit: a group of people; an organization; a business firm or concern.

Paine, Thomas: (1737–1809) political philosopher and author. Paine emigrated to America from England in 1774. In 1776 he published a pamphlet (*Common Sense*) urging immediate declaration of independence, which had wide circulation and great influence in concentrating sentiment in favor of immediate independence.

paucity: smallness of quantity; scarcity; scantiness.

Petrillo: James Caesar Petrillo (1892–1984), president of the American Federation of Musicians from 1940 to 1958. Petrillo organized several strikes—often without the support of public opinion—against radio, television and recording companies in order to strengthen the organization of his union and to combat increased use of technological devices which created less employment for musicians.

pilots: preliminary or experimental trials or tests.

pitch: comparative height or intensity of any quality or attribute; point or position on an ideal scale; degree, elevation, stage, status, level.

pomposity: the quality of being pompous, characterized by an exaggerated display of self-importance or dignity; boastfulness; arrogance.

pompous robes: literally, apparel or dress characterized by a pretentious or conspicuous display of dignity or importance in an attempt to impress others. Used figuratively in this sense.

post: a position, job or duty to which a person is assigned or appointed; an assigned area of responsibility and action in an organization which is supervised in part by an executive.

postulated: put forward as a reality.

protocol: the code of ceremonial forms and courtesies, of precedence, etc., accepted as proper and correct in official dealings. For example, in the navy, there are certain courtesies which a junior officer observes in dealing with senior officers, including how to address senior officers, when to salute, when to remove the cap, etc. The standard form for a business letter or contract would also be an example of protocol.

psychotic: characterized by or afflicted with psychosis. A *psychosis*, per psychiatry, is any major form of mental affliction or disease. In Scientology, a *psychotic* is classified as a person who is physically or mentally harmful to those about him out of proportion to the amount of use he is to them. Used figuratively in this sense.

punishment drive: pain, deprivation or other unpleasant consequence imposed on or experienced by an organism responding incorrectly under specific conditions so that, through avoidance, the desired learning or behavior becomes established.

rapacious: grasping; greedy.

reactive: irrational, reacting instead of acting.

reactive mind: that portion of a person's mind which works on a totally stimulus-response basis, which is not under his volitional control and which exerts force and the power of command over his awareness, purposes, thoughts, body and actions.

reality: the solid objects, the *real* things of life; the degree of agreement reached by two people. *See also* **ARC** in this glossary.

recalcitrant: "kicking" against constraint or restriction; obstinately disobedient or rebellious; unmanageable.

recasts: makes over; remodels.

recriminations: counter-accusations; accusations brought in turn by the accused against the accuser.

relative course: angle between the course of one's own ship and that of another adjacent ship.

Republic: the Weimar Republic, the existing government of Germany prior to Hitler's rise to power in the early '30s.

rhetoric: talk or writing that sounds grand or important but has little meaning.

Rockefeller: John Davison Rockefeller (1839–1937), American oil magnate; at one time was the world's richest man.

roller bearings: a system used in a machine in which a shaft turns with rollers, generally of steel, arranged in a ringlike track; used to reduce friction.

Rube Goldberg's machinery: cartoon mechanical devices of absurdly unnecessary complexity drawn by Rube Goldberg (1883–1970), American cartoonist.

Scientology: Scientology philosophy. It is the study and handling of the spirit in relationship to itself, universes and other life. Scientology means *scio,* knowing in the fullest sense of the word and *logos,* study. In itself the word means literally *knowing how to know.* Scientology is a "route," a way, rather than a dissertation or an assertive body of knowledge. Through its drills and studies one may find the truth for himself. The technology is therefore not expounded as something to believe, but something to *do.*

shunted: switched to another route or place.

silos: large bins used for the storage of loose materials. Used figuratively in this sense.

socialism: a theory or policy of social organization which aims at or advocates the ownership and control of the means of production, capital, land, property, etc., by the community as a whole, and their administration or distribution in the interests of all.

source-point: that from which something comes or develops; place of origin; cause. If you consider a river flowing to the sea, the place where it began would be the source-point or cause, and the place where it went into the sea would be the effect-point, and the sea would be the effect of the river.

specious: having a fair or attractive appearance or character, calculated to make a favorable impression on the mind, but in reality devoid of the qualities apparently possessed.

spots: determines (a location) precisely on either the ground or a map.

sprawl: spread out in a straggling or disordered fashion.

spurious: not genuine, authentic or true; not from the claimed, pretended or proper source; counterfeit.

Standard Oil: an oil company incorporated by John D. Rockefeller in 1870 which grew very rapidly, becoming one of the largest oil companies in the United States at the time.

St. Paul: (ca A.D. 3–68) Originally Saul, whose conversion to Christianity was attended by a vision. He became an apostle to the Gentiles, making several missionary journeys and founding many churches to which he sent letters which are now part of the New Testament. St. Paul was one of the greatest moral and spiritual teachers of his time.

tawdry: of the nature of cheap finery; showy or gaudy without real value.

temper: to soften or tone down.

tenor: the course of thought or meaning that runs through something written or spoken.

terminal: a point that receives, relays and sends communication; a man would be a terminal, but a post (position, job or duty to which a person is assigned) would also be a terminal.

terse: neatly or effectively precise; brief and full of substance or meaning.

tersest: most neatly or effectively concise; briefest while retaining substance or meaning.

theta: energy peculiar to life which acts upon material in the physical universe and animates it, mobilizes it and changes it; natural creative energy of a being which he has free to direct toward survival goals, especially when it manifests itself as useful, constructive communications. The term comes from the Greek letter *theta* (θ), which the Greeks used to represent *thought* or perhaps *spirit*. The broad definition of *theta* as used in Scientology is thought, life force, *élan vital*, the spirit, the soul.

third dynamic: the urge toward survival through a group of individuals or as a group. Any group or part of an entire class could be considered to be a part of the third dynamic. The school, the club, the team, the town, the nation are examples of groups. *See also* **dynamics** in this glossary.

3: the level 3.0 on the Tone Scale, conservatism. *See also* **Tone Scale** in this glossary, and the Tone Scale included in the Appendix, page 133.

tidal wave: any widespread or powerful movement, opinion or tendency; literally means a large destructive ocean wave produced by a seaquake (an earthquake on the ocean floor), hurricane or strong wind.

time file: a chronological file containing copies of the communications which have passed through the communication system and have been answered or complied with.

time machine: a series of baskets, one for each day of the week, used to keep track of an executive's orders and to report back to the executive either compliance or noncompliance with the order. A carbon copy of the order is placed in today's basket when it is received, and it is advanced one basket every morning. When compliance to the order is received, it is clipped to the order and sent to the issuing executive. If the order is not complied to within a week, it falls off the time machine by appearing in the basket being emptied on that day. The copy of the order is then returned to the issuing executive to show his order has not been complied with, so that he can handle the situation.

tone: a level of emotion as given on the Tone Scale. *See also* **Tone Scale** in this glossary.

Tone Scale: a scale, in Scientology, which shows the emotional tones of a person. These, ranged from the highest to the lowest, are, in part, serenity, enthusiasm (as we proceed downward), conservatism, boredom, antagonism, anger, covert hostility, fear, grief, apathy. An arbitrary numerical value is given to each level on the scale. (*See Appendix, page 133.*) There are many aspects of the *Tone Scale* and using it makes possible the prediction of human behavior. For further information on the Tone Scale, read the book *Science of Survival* by L. Ron Hubbard.

Townsend, Francis: (1867–1960), American physician who originated legislation in 1934 to provide old-age pensions (Townsend plan) in the United States. Although bills to enact the Townsend plan were continually defeated, its popularity contributed to passage of Social Security legislation.

two-way communication: the normal cycle of a communication between two people, which works as follows: Joe, having originated a communication, and having completed it, may then wait for Bill to originate a communication to Joe, thus completing the remainder of the two-way cycle of communication.

tycoon: a businessperson of great wealth and power.

tyrant: any person who exercises authority in an oppressive manner; cruel master.

unionism: the system, principles or methods of groups designed to protect and advance the interests of wage and salary workers, particularly in large industrial and commercial concerns of the Western world.

United States Army Signal Corps: a branch of the army responsible for military communications, meteorological studies and related work.

USS: United States Senate.

usurp: appropriate wrongly to oneself (a right, prerogative, etc.).

usurpation: the act of usurping (wrongly appropriating) another's rights, privileges, etc.; an instance of encroachment on or upon (liberty, etc.).

Valhalla: (*mythology*) the great hall where the god Odin receives and feasts the souls of heroes fallen bravely in battle. The word literally means *hall of the slain.*

verbose: using or containing too many words; wordy; long-winded.

whopping: extremely, exceedingly.

windy: full of talk or verbiage (an excess of words beyond those needed to express concisely what is meant); talkative; long-winded.

Wirephoto: (*trademark*) a device for transmitting photographs over distances by wire, as in a telegraph system.

wolf packs: groups of submarines operating together in hunting down and attacking enemy convoys.

yardarm: the outer portion of a yard. A *yard* is a large wooden or metal rod crossing the masts of a ship horizontally or diagonally, from which a sail is set. The *yardarms* are the end sections of the yard on either side of the ship.

Index

Books and Tapes by L. Ron Hubbard

Basic Executive Books

You've read *How to Live Though an Executive*. Now get the rest of the Basic Executive Books Package for even more information to help you to succeed in business. These books are available individually or as a set, complete with an attractive slipcase.

The Problems of Work • Work plays a big part in the game of life. Do you really enjoy your work? Are you certain of your job security? Would you like the increased personal satisfaction of doing your work well? This is the book that shows exactly how to achieve these things and more. The game of life—and within it, the game of work—can be enjoyable and rewarding.

Introduction to Scientology Ethics • A complete knowledge of ethics is vital to anyone's success in life. Without knowing and applying the information in this book, success is only a matter of luck or chance. That is not much to look forward to. This book contains the answers to questions like, "How do I know when a decision is right or wrong?" "How can I predictably improve things around me?" The powerful ethics technology of L. Ron Hubbard is your way to ever-increasing survival.

Advanced Executive Materials

Organization Executive Course • The Organization Executive Course volumes contain organizational technology never before known to man. This is not just how a Scientology organization works; this is how the operation of *any* organization, *any* activity, can be improved. A person knowing the data in these volumes fully, and applying it, could completely reverse any downtrend in a company—or even a country!

Management Series Volumes 1 and 2 • These books contain technology that anyone who works with management in any way must know completely to be a true success. Contained in these books are such subjects as data evaluation, the technology of how to organize any area for maximum production and expansion, how to handle personnel, the actual technology of public relations and much more.

Modern Management Technology Defined: Hubbard Dictionary of Administration and Management • Here's a real breakthrough in the subject of administration and management! Eighty-six hundred words are defined for greater understanding of any business situation. Clear, precise Scientology definitions describe many previously baffling phenomena and bring truth, sanity and understanding to the often murky field of business management.

Basic Scientology Books

The Basic Scientology Books Package contains the knowledge you need to be able to improve conditions in life. These books are available individually or as a set, complete with an attractive slipcase.

Scientology: The Fundamentals of Thought • Improve life *and* make a better world with this easy-to-read book that lays out the fundamental truths about life and thought. No such knowledge has ever before existed, and no such results have ever before been attainable as those which can be reached by the use of this knowledge. Equipped with this book alone, one could perform seeming miracles in changing the states of health, ability and intelligence of people. This *is* how life works. This *is* how you change men, women and children for the better, and attain greater personal freedom.

A New Slant on Life • Have you ever asked yourself who am I? What am I? This book of articles by L. Ron Hubbard answers these all-too-common questions. This is knowledge one can use every day—for a new, more confident and happier slant on life!

Scientology 0-8: The Book of Basics • What is life? Did you know an individual can create space, energy and time? Here are the basics of life itself, and the secrets of becoming cause over any area of your life. Discover how you can use the data in this book to achieve your goals.

Basic Dictionary of Dianetics and Scientology • Compiled from the works of L. Ron Hubbard, this convenient dictionary contains the terms and expressions needed by anyone learning Dianetics and Scientology technology. And a *special bonus*—an easy-to-read Scientology organizing board chart that shows you who to contact for services and information at your nearest Scientology organization.

OT[1] Library Package

All the following books contain the knowledge of a spiritual being's relationship to this universe and how his abilities to

---

1. **OT:** abbreviation for **Operating Thetan,** a state of beingness. It is a being "at cause over matter, energy, space, time, form and life." *Operating* comes from "able to operate without dependency on things," and *thetan* is the Greek letter *theta* (θ), which the Greeks used to represent *thought* or perhaps *spirit*, to which an *n* is added to make a noun in the modern style used to create words in engineering. It is also θ^n or "theta to the nth degree," meaning unlimited or vast.

operate successfully in it can be restored. You can get all of these books individually or in a set, complete with an attractive slipcase.

Scientology 8-80 • What are the laws of life? We are all familiar with physical laws such as the law of gravity, but what laws govern life and thought? L. Ron Hubbard answers the riddles of life and its goals in the physical universe.

Scientology 8-8008 • Get the basic truths about your nature as a spiritual being and your relationship to the physical universe around you. Here, L. Ron Hubbard describes procedures designed to increase your abilities to heights previously only dreamed of.

Scientology: A History of Man • A fascinating look at the history of the human race—revolutionary concepts guaranteed to intrigue you and challenge many basic assumptions about man's true power, potential and abilities.

The Creation of Human Ability • This book contains processes designed to restore the power of a being over his own considerations and thoughts, to understand the nature of his beingness, to free his self-determinism and much, much more.

Basic Dianetics Books

The Basic Dianetics Books Package is your complete guide to the inner workings of the mind. You can get all of these books individually or in a set, complete with an attractive slipcase.

Dianetics: The Modern Science of Mental Health • Acclaimed as the most effective self-help book ever published. Dianetics technology has helped millions reach new heights of freedom and ability. Millions of copies are sold every year! Discover the source of mental barriers that prevent you from achieving your goals—and how to handle them!

The Dynamics of Life • Break through the barriers to your happiness. This is the first book Ron wrote detailing the startling principles behind Dianetics—facts so powerful they can change forever the way you look at yourself and your potentials. Discover how you can use the powerful basic principles in this book to blast through the barriers of your mind and gain full control over your success, future and happiness.

Self Analysis • The complete do-it-yourself handbook for anyone who wants to improve their abilities and success potential. Use the simple, easy-to-learn techniques in *Self Analysis* to build self-confidence and reduce stress.

Dianetics: The Evolution of a Science • It is estimated that we use less than ten percent of our mind's potential. What stops us from developing and using the full potential of our minds? *Dianetics: The Evolution of a Science* is L. Ron Hubbard's incredible story of how he discovered the reactive mind and how he developed the keys to unlock its secrets. Get this firsthand account of what the mind really is, and how you can release its hidden potential.

Dianetics Graduate Books

These books by L. Ron Hubbard give you detailed knowledge of how the mind works—data you can use to help yourself and others break out of the traps of life. While you can get these books individually, the Dianetics Graduate Books Package can also be purchased as a set, complete with an attractive slipcase.

Science of Survival • If you ever wondered why people act the way they do, you'll find this book a wealth of information. It's vital to anyone who wants to understand others and improve personal relationships. *Science of Survival* is built around a remarkable chart—The Hubbard Chart of Human Evaluation. With it you can understand and predict other people's behavior and reactions and greatly increase your control over your own life. This is a valuable handbook that can make a difference between success and failure on the job and in life.

Dianetics 55! • Your success in life depends on your ability to communicate. Do you know a formula exists for communication? Learn the rules of better communication that can help you live a more fulfilling life. Here, L. Ron Hubbard deals with the fundamental principles of communication and how you can master these to achieve your goals.

Advanced Procedure and Axioms • For the *first* time the basics of thought and the physical universe have been codified into a set of fundamental laws, signaling an entirely new way to view and approach the subjects of man, the physical universe and even life itself.

Handbook for Preclears • Written as an advanced personal workbook, *Handbook for Preclears* contains easily done processes to help you overcome the effect of times you were not in control of your life, times that your emotions were a barrier to your success and much more. Completing all the fifteen auditing steps contained in this book sets you up for really being in *control* of your environment and life.

Child Dianetics • Here is a revolutionary new approach to rearing children with Dianetics auditing techniques. Find out how you can help your child achieve greater confidence, more self-reliance, improved learning rate and a happier, more loving relationship with you.

Notes on the Lectures of L. Ron Hubbard • Compiled from his fascinating lectures given shortly after the publication of

Dianetics, this book contains some of the first material Ron ever released on the ARC triangle and the Tone Scale, and how these discoveries relate to auditing.

Other Scientology Books

Purification: An Illustrated Answer to Drugs • Do toxins and drugs hold down your ability to think clearly? What is the Purification program and how does it work? How can harmful chemical substances be gotten out of the body? Our society is ridden by abuse of drugs, alcohol and medicine that reduce one's ability to think clearly. Find out what can be done in this introduction to the Purification program.

The Miracle of Purification • This book contains all the information on L. Ron Hubbard's Purification program. This is the only program of its kind in existence that has been found to clean the residues of drugs, toxins and elements harmful to human bodies out of them! Drugs and chemicals can stop a person's ability to improve himself or just to live life. This book describes the program which can make it possible to start living again.

All About Radiation • Can the effects of radiation exposure be avoided or reduced? What exactly would happen in the event of an atomic explosion? Get the answers to these and many other questions in this illuminating book. *All About Radiation* describes observations and discoveries concerning the physical and mental effects of radiation and the possibilities for handling them. Get the real facts on the subject of radiation and its effects.

Have You Lived Before This Life? • This is the book that sparked a flood of interest in the ancient puzzle: Does man live only one life? The answer lay in mystery, buried until L. Ron Hubbard's researches unearthed the truth. Actual case histories of people recalling past lives in auditing tell the tale.

Dianetics and Scientology Technical Dictionary • This dictionary is your indispensable guide to the words and ideas of Scientology and Dianetics technologies—technologies which can help you increase your know-how and effectiveness in life. Over three thousand words are defined—including a new understanding of vital words like *life, love* and *happiness* as well as Scientology terms.

Background and Ceremonies of the Church of Scientology • Discover the beautiful and inspiring ceremonies of the Church of Scientology, and its fascinating religious and historical background. This book contains the illuminating Creed of the Church, church services, sermons and ceremonies, many as originally given in person by L. Ron Hubbard, Founder of Scientology.

What Is Scientology? • Scientology applied religious philosophy has attracted great interest and attention since its beginning. What is Scientology philosophy? What can it accomplish— and why are so many people from all walks of life proclaiming its effectiveness? Find the answers to these questions and many others in *What Is Scientology?*

Introductory and Demonstration Processes and Assists • How can you help someone increase his enthusiasm for living? How can you improve someone's self-confidence on the job? Here are basic Scientology processes you can use to help others deal with life and living.

Volunteer Minister's Handbook • This is a big, practical how-to-do-it book to give a person the basic knowledge on how to help self and others through the rough spots in life. It consists of twenty-one sections—each one covering important situations in life, such as drug and alcohol problems, study difficulties, broken marriages, accidents and illnesses, a failing business, difficult children, and much more. This is the basic tool you need to help someone out of troubles, and bring about a happier life.

The Personal Achievement Series

There are nearly three thousand recorded lectures by L. Ron Hubbard on the subjects of Dianetics and Scientology. What follows is a sampling of these lectures, each known and loved the world over. All of these are presented in Clearsound state-of-the-art sound-recording technology, notable for its clarity and brilliance of reproduction.

Get all the Personal Achievement Series cassettes by L. Ron Hubbard listed below and ask your nearest Scientology church or organization or the publisher about future releases.

The Story of Dianetics and Scientology • In this lecture, L. Ron Hubbard shares with you his earliest insights into human nature and gives a compelling and often humorous account of his experiences. Spend an unforgettable time with Ron as he talks about the start of Dianetics and Scientology!

The Road to Truth • The road to truth has eluded man since the beginning of time. In this classic lecture, L. Ron Hubbard explains what this road actually is and why it is the only road one MUST travel all the way once begun. This lecture reveals the only road to higher levels of living.

Scientology and Effective Knowledge • Voyage to new horizons of awareness! *Scientology and Effective Knowledge* by L. Ron Hubbard can help you understand more about yourself and others. A fascinating tale of the beginnings of Dianetics and Scientology.

The Deterioration of Liberty • What do governments fear so much in a population that they amass weapons to defend themselves from people? Find out from Ron in this classic lecture.

Power of Choice and Self-Determinism • Man's ability to determine the course of his life depends on his ability to exercise his power of choice. Find out how you can increase your power of choice and self-determinism in life from Ron in this lecture.

Scientology and Ability • Ron points out that this universe is here because we perceive it and agree to it. Applying Scientology principles to life can bring new adventure to life and put you on the road to discovering better beingness.

The Hope of Man • Various men in history brought forth the idea that there was hope of improvement. But L. Ron Hubbard's discoveries in Dianetics and Scientology have made that hope a reality. Find out by listening to this lecture how Scientology has become man's one, true hope for his final freedom.

The Dynamics • In this lecture Ron gives incredible data on the dynamics: how man creates on them, what happens when a person gets stuck in just one, how wars relate to the third dynamic and much more.

Money • Ron talks in this classic lecture about that subject which makes or breaks men with the greatest of ease—money. Find out what money really is and gain greater control over your own finances.

Formulas for Success—*The Five Conditions* • How does one achieve real success? It sometimes appears that luck is the primary factor, but the truth of the matter is that natural laws exist which govern the conditions of life. These laws have been discovered by Ron, and in this lecture he gives you the exact steps to take in order to improve conditions in any aspect of your life.

Health and Certainty • You need certainty of yourself in order to achieve the success you want in life. In *Health and Certainty*, L. Ron Hubbard tells how you can achieve certainty and really be free to think for yourself. Get this tape now and start achieving your full potential!

Operation Manual for the Mind • Everybody has a mind—but who has an operation manual for it? This lecture reveals why man went on for thousands of years without understanding how his mind is supposed to work. The problem has been solved. Find out how with this tape.

Miracles • Why is it that man often loses to those forces he resists or opposes? Why can't an individual simply overcome obstacles in life and win? In the tape lecture *Miracles,* L. Ron Hubbard describes why one suffers losses in life. He also describes how a person can experience the miracles of happiness, self-fulfillment and winning at life. Get a copy today.

The Road to Perfection—*The Goodness of Man* • Unlike earlier practices that sought to "improve" man because he was "bad," Scientology assumes that you have *good* qualities that simply need to be *increased.* In *The Road to Perfection,* L. Ron Hubbard shows how workable this assumption really is—and how you can begin to use your mind, talents and abilities to the fullest. Get this lecture and increase your ability to handle life.

The Dynamic Principles of Existence • What does it take to survive in today's world? It's not something you learn much about in school. You have probably gotten a lot of advice about how to "get along." *Your survival right now is limited by the data you were given.* This lecture describes the dynamic principles of existence, and tells how you can use these principles to increase your success in all areas of life. Happiness and self-esteem *can* be yours. Don't settle for anything less.

Man: Good or Evil? • In this lecture, L. Ron Hubbard explores the greatest mystery that has confronted modern science and philosophy—the true nature of man's livingness and beingness. Is man simply a sort of wind-up doll or clock—or worse, an evil beast with no control of his cravings? Or is he capable of reaching higher levels of ability, awareness and happiness? Get this tape and find out the *real* answers.

Differences between Scientology and Other Studies • The most important questions in life are the ones you started asking as a child: What happens to a person when he dies? Is man basically good, or is he evil? What are the intentions of the world toward me? Did my mother and father really love me? What is love? Unlike other studies, which try to *force* you to think a certain way, Scientology enables you to find your own answers. Listen to this important lecture. It will put you on the road to true understanding and belief in yourself.

The Machinery of the Mind • We do a lot of things "automatically"—such as driving a car. But what happens when a person's mental machinery takes over and starts running him? In this fascinating lecture, L. Ron Hubbard gives you an understanding of what mental machinery really is, and how it can cause a person to lose control. You *can* regain your power of decision and be in full control of your life. Listen to this lecture and find out how.

The Affinity–Reality–Communication Triangle • Have you ever tried to talk to an angry man? Have you ever tried to get something across to someone who is really in fear? Have you ever known someone who was impossible to cheer up? Listen to this fascinating lecture by L. Ron Hubbard and learn how you can use the affinity-reality-communication triangle to resolve personal relationships. By using the data in this lecture, you can better understand others and live a happier life.

Increasing Efficiency • Inefficiency is a major barrier to success. How can you increase your efficiency? Is it a matter of changing your diet, or adjusting your working environment? These approaches have uniformly failed, because they overlook the most important element: *you*. L. Ron Hubbard has found those factors that *can* increase your efficiency, and he reveals it in this timely lecture. Get *Increasing Efficiency* now, and start achieving *your* full potential.

Man's Relentless Search • For countless centuries, man has been trying to find himself. Why does this quest repeatedly end in frustration and disappointment? What is he *really* looking for, and why can't he find it? For the real truth about man and life, listen to this taped lecture by L. Ron Hubbard, *Man's Relentless Search*. Restore your belief in yourself!

More advanced books and lectures are available. Contact your nearest organization or write directly to the publisher for a full catalog.

Improve
Your Business Skills
with
Extension Courses

Books by L. Ron Hubbard contain the knowledge needed to achieve success in any aspect of life from business to personal relationships. Now learn to take and *use* that knowledge to gain greater control of *your* life. Enroll on an extension course.

Each extension course package includes a lesson book with easy-to-understand instructions and all the lessons you will need to complete it. Each course can be done in the comfort of your own home or in your local Scientology organization. Your Extension Course Supervisor will review each lesson as you complete it (or mail it in if you do the course at home) and get the results right back to you. When you complete the course you get a beautiful certificate, suitable for framing.

The How to Live Though an Executive
Extension Course

Now there is a complete technology for any executive on how to handle the biggest drain on his time: communication. This technology is based on natural laws as factual as the law of gravity. Learn more about how the rules of communication can lead you and your business to success on the *How to Live Though an Executive Extension Course!*

The Problems of Work
Extension Course

Trying to handle a job and keep it can get to be a deadlier struggle with each working day. What are the secrets to increasing your enjoyment of work? How can you gain the personal satisfaction of doing your work well? Find the answers and apply them easily. Do *The Problems of Work Extension Course!*

The Introduction to Scientology Ethics
Extension Course

For the first time, man has a technology of ethics and a way to simply and predictably improve conditions in life. The *Introduction to Scientology Ethics Extension Course* helps you learn this miraculous technology and fully understand it so you can *use* it. Open a whole new realm of success in your life with the *Introduction to Scientology Ethics Extension Course.*

Enroll on an Extension Course for an
L. Ron Hubbard Book Today!

For information, enrollment and prices of these extension courses and the books they accompany, contact the Public Registrar at your nearest Church of Scientology. (A complete list of Scientology churches and organizations is provided at the back of this book.)

For more information about Scientology or to order books and cassettes

Call: 1-800-334-LIFE
in the US and Canada

Is there such a thing as a hotline that doesn't believe in giving advice? What about a hotline for able individuals to help them solve their *own* problems?

"If we take a man and keep giving him advice," L. Ron Hubbard has said, "we don't necessarily wind up with a resolution of his problems. But if, on the other hand, we put him in a position where he had higher intelligence, where his reaction time was better, where he could confront life better, where he could identify the factors in his life more easily, then he's in a position where he can solve his own problems."

Call the unique new hotline and referral service with operators trained in Scientology technology. Callers find someone they can trust to talk to about a problem, and they are referred to their nearest Scientology church or organization for more information if they are interested.

You can also order books and cassettes by L. Ron Hubbard by calling this number.

**Call this toll-free number
7 days a week
from 9 A.M. to 11 P.M. Pacific Standard Time.**

Get Your Free Catalog
of Knowledge on
How to Improve Life

L. Ron Hubbard's books and tapes increase your ability to understand yourself and others. His works give you the practical know-how you need to improve your life and the lives of your family and friends.

Many more materials by L. Ron Hubbard are available than have been covered in the pages of this book. A free catalog of these materials is available on request.

Write for your free catalog today!

Bridge Publications, Inc.
4751 Fountain Avenue
Los Angeles, California 90029

NEW ERA Publications International, ApS
Store Kongensgade 55
1264 Copenhagen K, Denmark

"I am always happy to hear from my readers."

L. Ron Hubbard

These were the words of L. Ron Hubbard, who was always very interested in hearing from his friends and readers. He made a point of staying in communication with everyone he came in contact with over his fifty-year career as a professional writer, and he had thousands of fans and friends that he corresponded with all over the world.

The publishers of L. Ron Hubbard's works wish to continue this tradition and welcome letters and comments from you, his readers, both old and new.

Additionally, the publishers will be happy to send you information on anything you would like to know about Ron, his extraordinary life and accomplishments and the vast number of books he has written.

Any message addressed to the Author's Affairs Director at Bridge Publications will be given prompt and full attention.

Bridge Publications, Inc.
4751 Fountain Avenue
Los Angeles, California 90029
USA

Church and Organization Address List

Kansas City
Church of Scientology
3619 Broadway
Kansas City, Missouri 64111

Las Vegas
Church of Scientology
846 East Sahara Avenue
Las Vegas, Nevada 89104

Church of Scientology
Celebrity Centre Las Vegas
1100 South 10th Street
Las Vegas, Nevada 89104

Long Island
Church of Scientology
330 Fulton Avenue
Hempstead, New York 11550

Los Angeles and vicinity
Church of Scientology
4810 Sunset Boulevard
Los Angeles, California 90027

Church of Scientology
1451 Irvine Boulevard
Tustin, California 92680

Church of Scientology
263 East Colorado Boulevard
Pasadena, California 91101

Church of Scientology
10335 Magnolia Boulevard
North Hollywood, California 91601

Church of Scientology
American Saint Hill Organization
1413 North Berendo Street
Los Angeles, California 90027

Church of Scientology
American Saint Hill Foundation
1413 North Berendo Street
Los Angeles, California 90027

Church of Scientology
Advanced Organization of
  Los Angeles
1306 North Berendo Street
Los Angeles, California 90027

Church of Scientology
Celebrity Centre International
5930 Franklin Avenue
Hollywood, California 90028

Miami
Church of Scientology
120 Giralda Avenue
Coral Gables, Florida 33134

Minneapolis
Church of Scientology
3019 Minnehaha Avenue
Minneapolis, Minnesota 55406

New Haven
Church of Scientology
909 Whalley Avenue
New Haven, Connecticut 06515

New York City
Church of Scientology
227 West 46th Street
New York City, New York 10036

Church of Scientology
Celebrity Centre New York
65 East 82nd Street
New York City, New York 10028

Orlando
Church of Scientology
710-A East Colonial Drive
Orlando, Florida 32803

Philadelphia
Church of Scientology
1315 Race Street
Philadelphia, Pennsylvania 19107

Phoenix
Church of Scientology
4450 North Central Avenue, Suite 102
Phoenix, Arizona 85012

Portland
Church of Scientology
323 SW Washington
Portland, Oregon 97204

Church of Scientology
Celebrity Centre Portland
709 Southwest Salmon Street
Portland, Oregon 97205

Sacramento
Church of Scientology
825 15th Street
Sacramento, California 95814

San Diego
Church of Scientology
701 "C" Street
San Diego, California 92101

San Francisco
Church of Scientology
83 McAllister Street
San Francisco, California 94102

San Jose
Church of Scientology
80 E. Rosemary
San Jose, California 95112

Santa Barbara
Church of Scientology
524 State Street
Santa Barbara, California 93101

Seattle
Church of Scientology
2004 Westlake Avenue
Seattle, Washington 98121

St. Louis
Church of Scientology
9510 Page Boulevard
St. Louis, Missouri 63132

Tampa
Church of Scientology
4809 North Armenia Avenue
Suite 215
Tampa, Florida 33603

Washington, DC
Founding Church of Scientology
2125 "S" Street NW
Washington, DC 20008

Canada

Edmonton
Church of Scientology
10349 82nd Avenue
Edmonton, Alberta
Canada T6E 1Z9

Kitchener
Church of Scientology
8 Water Street North
Kitchener, Ontario
Canada N2H 5A5

Montréal
Church of Scientology
4489 Papineau Street
Montréal, Québec
Canada H2H 1T7

Ottawa
Church of Scientology
150 Rideau Street, 2nd Floor
Ottawa, Ontario
Canada K1N 5X6

Québec
Church of Scientology
226 St-Joseph est
Québec, Québec
Canada G1K 3A9

Toronto
Church of Scientology
696 Yonge Street
Toronto, Ontario
Canada M4Y 2A7

Vancouver
Church of Scientology
401 West Hastings Street
Vancouver, British Columbia
Canada V6B 1L5

Winnipeg
Church of Scientology
Suite 125—388 Donald Street
Winnipeg, Manitoba
Canada R3B 2J4

United Kingdom

Birmingham
Church of Scientology
60/62 Constitution Hill
Birmingham
England B5 4TD

Brighton
Church of Scientology
Dukes Arcade, Top Floor
Dukes Street
Brighton, Sussex, England

East Grinstead
Saint Hill Foundation
Saint Hill Manor
East Grinstead, West Sussex
England RH19 4JY

Advanced Organization Saint Hill
Saint Hill Manor
East Grinstead, West Sussex
England RH19 4JY

Edinburgh
Hubbard Academy of Personal
    Independence
20 Southbridge
Edinburgh, Scotland EH1 1LL

London
Church of Scientology
68 Tottenham Court Road
London, England W1P 0BB

Manchester
Church of Scientology
258 Deansgate
Manchester, England M3 4BG

Plymouth
Church of Scientology
41 Ebrington Street
Plymouth, Devon
England PL4 9AA

Sunderland
Church of Scientology
51 Fawcett Street
Sunderland, Tyne and Wear
England SR1 1RS

Austria

Vienna
Church of Scientology
Schottenfeldgasse 13–15
1070 Wien, Austria

Vienna South
Church of Scientology
Celebrity Centre
Senefelderg. 11/5
1100 Wien, Austria

Belgium

Brussels
Church of Scientology
45A, rue de l'Ecuyer
1000 Bruxelles, Belgium

Denmark

Aarhus
Church of Scientology
Guldsmedegade 17, 2
8000 Aarhus C., Denmark

Copenhagen
Church of Scientology
Store Kongensgade 55
1264 Copenhagen K, Denmark

Church of Scientology
Vesterbrogade 66
1620 Copenhagen V, Denmark

Church of Scientology
Advanced Organization Saint Hill
    for Europe and Africa
Jernbanegade 6
1608 Copenhagen V, Denmark

France

Angers
Church of Scientology
10–12, rue Max Richard
49000 Angers, France

Clermont-Ferrand
Church of Scientology
2 Pte rue Giscard de la Tour Fondue
63000 Clermont-Ferrand, France

Lyon
Church of Scientology
3, place des Capucins
69001 Lyon, France

Paris
Church of Scientology
65, rue de Dunkerque
75009 Paris, France

Church of Scientology
Celebrity Centre Paris
69, rue Legendre
75017 Paris, France

St. Etienne
Church of Scientology
24, rue Marengo
42000 St. Etienne, France

Germany

Berlin
Church of Scientology e.V.
Sponholzstrasse 51/52
1000 Berlin 41, Germany

Düsseldorf
Church of Scientology
Friedrichstrasse 28
4000 Düsseldorf, West Germany

Church of Scientology
Celebrity Centre Düsseldorf
Grupellostr. 28
4000 Düsseldorf, West Germany

Frankfurt
Church of Scientology
Darmstadter Landstrasse 119–125
6000 Frankfurt/Main, West Germany

Hamburg
Church of Scientology e.V.
Steindamm 63
2000 Hamburg 1, West Germany

Church of Scientology
Celebrity Centre Hamburg
Mönckebergstrasse 5/IV
2000 Hamburg 1
West Germany

Hannover
Church of Scientology
Bödekerstrasse 96
3000 Hannover 1, West Germany

Munich
Church of Scientology e.V.
Beichstrasse 12
D-8000 München 40, West Germany

Greece

Athens
Applied Philosophy Center of Greece
(K.E.F.E.)
Ippokratous 175B
114 72 Athens, Greece

Israel

Tel Aviv
Scientology and Dianetics College
7 Salomon Street
Tel Aviv 66023, Israel

Italy

Brescia
Church of Scientology
Dei Tre Laghi
Via Fratelli Bronzetti N. 20
25125 Brescia, Italy

Milan
Church of Scientology
Via Abetone, 10
20137 Milano, Italy

Monza
Church of Scientology
Via Cavour, 5
20052 Monza, Italy

Novara
Church of Scientology
Corso Cavallotti No. 7
28100 Novara, Italy

Nuoro
Church of Scientology
Corso Garibaldi, 108
08100 Nuoro, Italy

Padua
Church of Scientology
Via Mameli 1/5
35131 Padova, Italy

Pordenone
Church of Scientology
Via Montereale, 10/C
33170 Pordenone, Italy

Rome
Church of Scientology
Via di San Vito, 11
00185 Roma, Italy

Turin
Church of Scientology
Via Guarini, 4
10121 Torino, Italy

Verona
Church of Scientology
Vicolo Chiodo No. 4/A
37121 Verona, Italy

Netherlands

Amsterdam
Church of Scientology
Nieuwe Zijds Voorburgwal 271
1012 RL Amsterdam, Netherlands

Norway

Oslo
Church of Scientology
Storgata 9
0155 Oslo 1, Norway

Portugal

Lisbon
Instituto de Dianética
Rua Actor Taborda 39–4°
1000 Lisboa, Portugal

Spain

Barcelona
Dianética
Calle Pau Claris 85, Principal 1ª
08010 Barcelona, Spain

Madrid
Asociación Civil de Dianética
Montera 20, Piso 1° DCHA
28013 Madrid, Spain

Sweden

Göteborg
Church of Scientology
Odinsgatan 8
411 03 Göteborg, Sweden

Malmö
Church of Scientology
Simrishamnsgatan 10
21423 Malmö, Sweden

Stockholm
Church of Scientology
Kammakargatan 46
S-111 60 Stockholm, Sweden

Switzerland

Basel
Church of Scientology
Herrengrabenweg 56
4054 Basel, Switzerland

Bern
Church of Scientology
Schulhausgasse 12
3113 Rubigen
Bern, Switzerland

Geneva
Church of Scientology
9 Route de Saint-Julien
1227 Carouge
Genève, Switzerland

Lausanne
Church of Scientology
10, rue de la Madeleine
1003 Lausanne, Switzerland

Zürich
Church of Scientology
Badenerstrasse 294
CH-8004 Zürich, Switzerland

Australia

Adelaide
Church of Scientology
24 Waymouth Street
Adelaide, South Australia 5000
Australia

Brisbane
Church of Scientology
2nd Floor, 106 Edward Street
Brisbane, Queensland 4000
Australia

Canberra
Church of Scientology
Suite 16, 108 Bunda Street
Canberra Civic
A.C.T. 2601, Australia

Melbourne
Church of Scientology
44 Russell Street
Melbourne, Victoria 3000
Australia

Perth
Church of Scientology
39–41 King Street
Perth, Western Australia 6000
Australia

Sydney
Church of Scientology
201 Castlereagh Street
Sydney, New South Wales 2000
Australia

Church of Scientology
Advanced Organization Saint Hill
    Australia, New Zealand and
    Oceania
19–37 Greek Street
Glebe, New South Wales 2037
Australia

Japan

Tokyo
Scientology Tokyo Org
101 Toyomi Nishi Gotanda Heights
2-13-5 Nishi Gotanda
Shinagawa-Ku
Tokyo, Japan 141

New Zealand

Auckland
Church of Scientology
2nd Floor, 44 Queen Street
Auckland 1, New Zealand

Africa

Bulawayo
Church of Scientology
74, Abercorn Street
Bulawayo, Zimbabwe

Cape Town
Church of Scientology
5 Beckham Street
Gardens
Cape Town 8001, South Africa

Durban
Church of Scientology
57 College Lane
Durban 4001, South Africa

Harare
Church of Scientology
First Floor State Lottery Building
P.O. Box 3524
Corner Speke Avenue and
    Julius Nyerere Way
Harare, Zimbabwe

Johannesburg
Church of Scientology
Security Building, 2nd Floor
95 Commissioner Street
Johannesburg 2001, South Africa

Church of Scientology
101 Huntford Building
40 Hunter Street
Cnr. Hunter & Fortesque Roads
Yeoville 2198
Johannesburg, South Africa

Port Elizabeth
Church of Scientology
2 St. Christopher
27 Westbourne Road
Port Elizabeth 6001, South Africa

Pretoria
Church of Scientology
"Die Meent Arcade,"
    2nd Level, Shop 43b
266 Pretorius Street
Pretoria 0002, South Africa

Latin America

Colombia

Bogotá
Centro Cultural de Dianética
Carrera 19 No. 39–55
Apartado Aereo 92419
Bogotá, D.E. Colombia

Mexico

Estado de México
Instituto Technologico de Dianética,
    A.C.
Londres 38, 5th Floor
Col. Juarez, México D.F.

Guadalajara
Organización Cultural Dianética de
    Guadalajara, A.C.
Av. Lopez Mateos Nte. 329
Sector Hidalgo
Guadalajara, Jalisco, México

Mexico City
Asociación Cultural Dianética, A.C.
Hermes No. 46
Colonia Crédito Constructor
03940 México 19, D.F.

Instituto de Filosofia Aplicada, A.C.
Durango #105
Colonia Roma
06700 México D.F.

Instituto de Filosofia Aplicada, A.C.
Plaza Rio de Janeiro No. 52
Colonia Roma
06700 México D.F.

Organización, Desarrollo y
  Dianética, A.C.
Providencia 1000
Colonia Del Valle
C.P. 03100 México D.F.

Centro de Dianética Polanco
Insurgentes Sur 536, 1er piso
  Esq. Nogales
Colonia Roma Sur C.P.
06700 México D.F.

Venezuela

Valencia
Asociación Cultural Dianética de
  Venezuela, A.C.
Ave. 101 No. 150–23
Urbanizacion La Alegria
Apartado Postal 833
Valencia, Venezuela

To obtain any books or cassettes by L. Ron Hubbard which are not available at your local organization, contact any of the following publishers:

Bridge Publications, Inc.
4751 Fountain Avenue
Los Angeles, California 90029

Continental Publications Liaison Office
696 Yonge Street
Toronto, Ontario
Canada M4Y 2A7

NEW ERA Publications International
  ApS
Store Kongensgade 55
1264 Copenhagen K, Denmark

Era Dinámica Editores, S.A. de C.V.
Alabama 105
Colonia Nápoles
C.P. 03810 México, D.F.

NEW ERA Publications, Ltd.
78 Holmethorpe Avenue
Redhill, Surrey RH1 2NL
United Kingdom

N.E. Publications Australia Pty. Ltd.
2 Verona Street
Paddington, New South Wales 2021
Australia

Continental Publications Pty. Ltd.
P.O. Box 27080
Benrose 2011
South Africa

NEW ERA Publications Italia Srl
Via L.G. Columella, 12
20128 Milano, Italy

NEW ERA Publications GmbH
Otto—Hahn—Strasse 25
6072 Dreieich 1, Germany

NEW ERA Publications France
111, boulevard de Magenta
75010 Paris, France

New Era Publications España, S.A.
C/De la Paz, 4/1° dcha
28012 Madrid, Spain

New Era Japan
5-4-5-803 Nishigotanda
Shinagawa-Ku
Tokyo, Japan 141